Let Us Abide

Let Us Abide

Judson Cornwall

FLEMING H. REVELL COMPANY
OLD TAPPAN, NEW JERSEY

Library of Congress Cataloging in Publication Data

Cornwall, E   Judson.
Let us abide.

1. Christian life—1960– I. Title.
BV4501.2.C678   248′.4   77–23143
ISBN 0–8007–0858–X

Acknowledgments

Traveling almost continuously as I do while still sharing responsibility as an elder in a local church, it would be impossible to write a book without the capable assistance of others. I would like to thank my two secretaries who typed and retyped the manuscript as repeated revisions were made: Laurel Watson, on the West Coast who has served me as a secretary for many years, and Mel Webber, on the East Coast who has been willing to set aside almost everything to help meet deadlines.

Thanks, also, to the Reverend John Romaine for the hours he invested in going through the first draft, editing, suggesting, and outlining the material for me.

Midway through this work I became convinced that I could not write. In near desperation I took a course in writing, and God, in His foreknowledge, arranged for me to secure a good Christian instructor who helped me find my major weaknesses in writing while rekindling my courage to keep trying. This book would not have been written without the encouragement of Emalene Shepherd. Thanks.

And my most particular thanks go to my wife, Eleanor, who sacrificed several hundred hours of companionship so I could write this book during my short times at home. She has been a cooperative assistant during the entire time of writing.

Contents

Preface

My book *Let Us Praise* quite naturally opened many doors for me to minister on praise. I found it exciting to bring new groups of people into a public expression of praise unto God. After a while I began to have repeat invitations to some of these groups and observed, rather sadly, that they had not maintained the level of praise that I had brought them into. It did not seem to be lack of desire or necessarily weakness of leadership, but they seemed to lack the relationship with God required to maintain a life of praise.

The more I pondered the situation, the keener my awareness became that there was a need for an intimate fellowship and relationship with God and that praise must always be the outgrowth of such a relationship, not the producer of it.

As I listened to Christians talk of their walk in God, it seemed that they lived from one crisis experience to the next with deep, long valleys in between these mountaintops. This pattern did not seem to fit the life of our Lord Jesus or the apostles. I kept asking myself, "If David, with all of his mistakes and sins, could find an abiding experience in God, why can't we New Testament saints find one too?"

In retrospect I realized that I had come into some measure of abiding before I had broken into a life of praise. My praise was the outgrowth of that continuing relationship. As I broke the erratic crisis-oriented approach to God's presence and learned to abide in Him continually, my life did a spiritual turnaround and embraced praise and worship instead of petition and work.

When the two Psalms that form the backbone of this book opened to me, I began to share them in camp meetings and conferences. The truth was accepted with great rejoicing. Several conference grounds sold a record number of tapes that week. Many asked that I put the teaching into book form for permanent reference. It has taken me nearly a year to fulfill their requests, but here it is in all its weakness.

No book, no author, no preacher could ever exhaust the wealth of teaching the Bible offers on the subject of abiding. This book is neither exhaustive nor complete. I have chosen to be content to stay with the outline of Psalm 15, sharing the areas of adjustment we may need to make in our living pattern before we can come into a continuous relationship with our God. If even one reader is able to find that "secret place" and "abide under the shadow of the Almighty" as a result of this work, I shall feel amply rewarded.

Let Us Abide

I

Ascend or Abide?

It was a beautiful day for flying. The passing rain had washed the air thoroughly giving us a visibility of more than twenty miles. My window seat gave me a panoramic view of the Peninsula as the 727 roared into the skies, taking me on my way from Virginia to speak at a banquet in Pennsylvania.

In spite of this, I couldn't focus my attention on the scenery below. I was hungry—spiritually hungry. The past two weeks had been so full of activity in my local assembly that I had robbed myself of time in the Word. I was not only hungry, but I felt parched, desperately needing a touch of God's Spirit before speaking.

Seeing my seat partner straining to look out the window, I volunteered to trade seats with him, insisting that I was going to read anyway. After my seat belt was refastened, I slipped my Bible out of its case and began to read in the Psalms. I always start reading in the Psalms unless I have predetermined to read a definite portion. Within minutes I felt a refreshing in my spirit. Once again I was able to identify with the Psalmist as he poured out his emotions to God.

Just before landing at National Airport in Washington, D.C., I noticed a strange parallel between Psalm 15 and Psalm 24. It is a parallel with a distinct contrast; yet each Psalm asks what a man must do to enter the presence of God.

By then the plane was parked at the gate. As usual, I had nearly a two-hour layover here in D.C.; so I went directly to United's Red Carpet Room, seated myself at a table, and began to write what I was seeing in the Word and hearing in my spirit.

I noted that Psalms 24:3 asks: "Who shall ascend into the hill of the LORD? or who shall stand in his holy place?" while Psalms 15:1 asks: "LORD, who shall abide in thy tabernacle? who shall dwell in thy holy hill?" One Psalm asks who may *ascend,* while the other asks who may *abide.* One expresses the desire to stand in God's presence for a moment, while the other, the desire to stay there.

I realized that this country, which was founded on religious principles and desire for religious freedom, has mercifully had repeated spiritual awakenings under the ministries of Charles Finney, Billy Sunday, Billy Graham, and others. Many millions of people were stirred by God's presence under their preaching.

Additionally, this generation has seen two major religious awakenings that have not been centered particularly around a man. In the early twentieth century a sovereign outpouring of God's Spirit brought forth a revival that produced the Pentecostal movements. In the mid-1900s another outpouring of God's Spirit created a great spiritual awakening in many of the mainline denominations as well as the Catholic church. This renewal, generally called the charismatic movement, is viewed by many church leaders as the greatest force for godliness that this generation has yet seen.

In each of these visitations many thousands have had a momentary standing in the presence of God. There has been a confrontation with the Divine. It has borne a variety of labels and has been accompanied with diverse manifestations, but it has been a definite experience of an individual finding himself in the presence of God for a short period of time in a crisis experience that was often mind-expanding and sensorially exhilarating.

So real was each confrontation as to effect changes in life-styles. Books were written about it, churches were built around it, and businessmen became missionaries because of it. God had confronted them, and they would never be the same again.

Some were confronted in a conversion experience, others in a healing grace, while still others were filled with the Spirit.

It is difficult to establish a pattern for it, for they came from all walks of life, from a diversity of religious heritages, and from sundry educational backgrounds. Some were seekers after God, as David the sweet singer of Israel, while others seemed more to be contenders with God, as Jacob; yet majestically they had been allowed to stand, however briefly, before the presence of Almighty God, not too unlike Moses who was hidden in the cleft of a rock while God passed and then was allowed a momentary glimpse of God's afterglow.

Apparently, no more able to find a pattern for it than I, the Psalmist asks God, "Who shall ascend into the hill of the LORD?" The answer is, "He that hath clean hands, and a pure heart; who hath not lifted up his soul unto vanity, nor sworn deceitfully." (Psalms 24:4).

Clean actions, clean motivations, and clean attitudes—inward and outward cleansing—seem to qualify a person for a crisis experience with God.

Each Hebrew in David's day would understand this, for before their priest could enter the holy place, he had to be cleansed by blood at the brazen altar and by water at the laver. The blood was for cleansing the guilt of sin—the inner impurity—and the water was for cleansing the defilement of the way and service. If cleansed within by blood and without by water, he was invited into the holy place for a veiled confrontation with God.

And so it is with the believer priest of today. "Let us draw near with a true heart in full assurance of faith, having our hearts sprinkled from an evil conscience, and our bodies washed with pure water" (Hebrews 10:22).

Both of these stations of cleansing in the outer court were provisions of grace. The sprinkling of the blood was done *for* them, and the washing at the laver was done *by* them, but the provision was grace, pure and simple.

No wonder, then, that Paul emphasized, "For by grace are ye saved through faith; and that not of yourselves: it is the gift of God: Not of works, lest any man should boast" (Ephesians 2:8, 9). Grace sought us when we were lost, bought us at a cost, and brought us to His cross while we were defiled, defiant, and degenerate sinners. "And the grace of our Lord was exceeding abundant with faith and love . . ." (1 Timothy 1:14).

Of his own crisis experience Paul said: "Howbeit for this cause I *obtained mercy,* that in me first Jesus Christ might shew forth all longsuffering, *for a pattern* to them which should hereafter believe on him to life everlasting" (1 Timothy 1:16, italics added). Paul was a religious zealot intent upon destroying all followers of "the way." By grace alone he was stopped in his tracks on the Damascus road and confronted by God in both vision and voice. It totally transformed him, so much so, that the aggressor became an apostle. It all started with the merciful and consequential confrontation.

When the ministry of grace has been received, the man is a candidate for a confrontation. It is not the visitor to the outer court, but the vicarious victor of the outer court ministries that experiences confrontation.

To see the grace of God and do nothing about it is as effective as refusing to take a doctor's prescription. The cure is at hand, but it needs to be applied. It is through faith in the finished work of Christ and identifying with His death that we are cleansed from the penalty, power, presence, and guilt of sin. Applying the work of the cross purges the heart from improper motivations and attitudes.

Similarly, it is by practical appropriation of the Word of God to all the details of our daily life that our actions are continually cleansed. It is not, therefore, *provided grace* that precipitates the crisis confrontation, but *applied grace*—grace that has been brought to bear on the inner and outer life. In 2 Corinthians 7:1 we are challenged: ". . . let us cleanse ourselves from all filthiness of the flesh and spirit. . . ."

We know that God cannot and will not have communion with a defiled saint but can and will cleanse him, for the blood of the cross secures our acceptance with God, and the water of the Word secures our purification.

So to David's question, "Who shall ascend?" God's answer is simply, "He who has applied My means of grace, who has met Me at the altar and the laver." Only the graced man will have a taste of the glory.

It was while Zacharias was tending the means of grace as a priest by burning incense upon the golden altar that the angel of the Lord appeared to him foretelling the birth of John the Baptist. (*See* Luke 1:8–13).

It was while Moses was tending the sheep—a beautiful foreshadowing of the coming Lamb of God—that a voice spoke to him out of the burning bush.

It seems that David also had his initial encounter with God while tending sheep, some of which would be sacrificed on the brazen altar.

Although the pattern has some exclusions—for all rules have their exceptions—most recent divine convergences have come to those who were consciously, or subconsciously, seeking God by one means or another. Some sought in prayer, others in the Word, and a few while observing the ceremonies and ordinances of their church. There was a heart crying out for release, or relief, that only God could bring when they found themselves standing in the presence of a saving God, a healing God, a baptizing God, a revealing God, or just a Holy God.

It may have been a brief encounter, but it was a glimpse into another world for them. It was their initial introduction into the Kingdom of God. They saw by their faith and felt by their senses things they had only imagined in their wildest flight of fancy. Their testimony of the experience was generally predicated upon what it had produced in them, such as: "I've been saved"; "I was healed"; or "The Lord filled me with His Holy Spirit. Even John the revela-

tor found it difficult to describe what he experienced in the Kingdom of God, while Paul declared that he heard "unspeakable
words, which it is not lawful [not possible] for a man to utter"
(*see* 2 Corinthians 12:4).

Recently a pastor friend of mine met a prospective student from
Africa at the airport in Toronto, Canada. As they drove through
that city, en route to the Bible school in New York State, the young
man exclaimed, "When I get home, they will never believe me
when I tell them what I am seeing."

Of course not! Our understanding of anything new must somehow fit the frame of reference of the old, or it comes into the realm
of revelation. So rather than try to explain the inexplicable, we
simply describe how we felt, what we heard, and how it affected
us.

As great and glorious as these crisis experiences are—these
golden moments when we seem to have glimpsed into eternity—
they are generally fleeting and are followed by the necessity of
returning to normal living, just as the disciples who had climbed
the mountain with Jesus to enter into the Transfiguration experience with Him had to come down to face the demonic son. These
spiritual highs are followed by great descents.

It is very much like a roller-coaster ride. These crisis experiences
seem to lift us, through little effort of our own, to heights never
before attained. But as soon as we reach the apex, we drop off the
other side. The trip down is so much faster than the trip up, and
the momentum of the descent forces us up again to a lesser height
from which we topple again, building momentum for a still lower
ascent. Eventually gravity and friction causes the roller coaster to
stop, usually at the same level it began.

We can either take another ride to a new crisis experience or stay
at the comfortable norm with a wealth of memories and an excited
set of emotions.

But is this what God has as an ultimate for His people? Does He
want us to ascend briefly to great spiritual heights only to return

to a standard norm? Are we to repeat the ritual of the Old Testament High Priest who annually took the products of the two altars —blood in a basin from the brazen altar and incense in a golden censer from the golden altar—and with great fear and trepidation entered into the divine presence of the holy of holies only to exit again in a few minutes grateful to be alive and thankful that next year it would be someone else's turn to go in?

No—a thousand times no! God's ultimate desire is intimate relationship with His people. God wants to walk and talk with us as He did with Adam. God wants us to enjoy His presence as Enoch did on his daily walks with God.

God wants to communicate with His people as He did with Moses and to sojourn with us as He did with Abraham. He yearns that we learn how to ascend out of ourselves into Himself. More than 160 times the Word declares that we are "in Christ." It is not that we have touched Him, stood before Him, or have had an experience with Him but that we can actually be *"In Him."*

When God made His first presentation of Himself to Israel at Mount Sinai, giving them the Ten Commandments, it produced terror in the hearts of the people. They sent word to Moses through their elders to tell God never to speak to them again; it would kill them if He spoke again. (*See* Deuteronomy 5:23–27.)

God's answer to Moses after he reclimbed the mountain with the request of the people is found in Leviticus 26:11–12: "And I will set my tabernacle among you. . . . And I will walk among you, and will be your God, and ye shall be my people."

When this verse is quoted in the New Testament the *among* becomes *in.* "I will dwell *in* them, and walk *in* them" (*see* 2 Corinthians 6:16, italics added).

It is not, therefore, God's ultimate plan simply to be our saviour, baptizer, healer, or even soon-to-come king. He is all of these in crisis relationship to us, but He desires continuous relationship. He wants to dwell among us, to walk in us, and to be our God in a most intimate form of communion.

A few months ago I received a phone call from my mother, telling me that she was getting remarried in a few weeks and asking if it would be convenient if she and her husband came to Virginia to share their honeymoon with me. I was thrilled to help arrange such a visit.

A week or so later I had a call from my oldest daughter, who was in Oregon, telling me that she desperately needed some time with her mother and father. We mailed her a ticket to come home.

The visit of my mother and daughter overlapped; so we explored some of the tourist spots together. We enjoyed Williamsburg, Jamestown, and the old battlefields around Yorktown and explored some of the unique restaurants of the area.

As the end of the visits neared, Mother told me that she would have memories enough to last for a lifetime but was looking forward to returning to Oregon.

My daughter also expressed her pleasure at what she had seen and had shared but asked, "Would it be possible to move back here and live close to you?" Her wish was granted within the month.

How much we are like that with God. He extends the means for us to enjoy a visit into His Kingdom. He shares some of its glories with us and favors us with heaven's best spiritual food. Some of us bid Him good-bye, assuring Him we will carry memories of this great visit to our dying day. Others ask if they can move in permanently. These are the ones who so delight the heart of God.

Although God strongly desires a continuous relationship, He gives us the brief crisis experiences, because pivotal relationships must precede the continuing experience. Until we have a foretaste, we'll never develop a taste for.

Look at Jacob who through no good act of his own had that paramount experience of the vision of angels ascending and descending from earth to heaven on a ladder—a vision of the glory of God such as few of us have yet seen. He did not experience it because he was a good man, for at this point he was a thief, a liar, a cheat, a charlatan, and a fugitive from his brother's wrath. Yet

God gave him a crisis experience and then let him go on. Because of this experience he had sufficient faith in God to withstand the years in which everything he had done to his father and his brother was done to him by his father's brother. In every area in which he had been a cheat, he found himself being cheated seven times over. After twenty-one years of this, he felt it might be good to go back to abide in the land where God had appeared to him.

It was on his way back that he had his second confrontation with God, which became a continuing experience. In this encounter he experienced a name change, a nature change, and a physical change. He walked a cripple the rest of his life, but he was crippled because of the intervention of God. He had to have the initial crisis experience to hold him steady during the subsequent dealings with God so that he could come into a continuing experience.

The same principle can be seen in the Exodus of the Israelites. First, there was the beautiful crisis experience of being exempted from the death of the firstborn in Egypt. Then came the climactic experience of the opened Red Sea followed by the sweetening of the bitter waters at Marah by casting the tree into the pond. Later came the opening of the rock for a water supply. The provision of nearly twenty trainloads of manna upon the early dew every morning was a momentous experience for them. It was a life-and-death encounter on a day-to-day basis.

It was only after a series of crucial, decisive supernatural interventions by God, founded totally upon grace and not upon their faith or even their desire (for most of these experiences came in the midst of their fear and anxiety), that God's voice came from Mount Sinai saying, "Welcome home, children. I am the Lord who brought you out, and I want relationship with you." So we understand that crisis experiences are intended to bring us into continuing relationship with God.

This pattern is also illustrated in the Old Testament sacrifices and ordinances. They were experience oriented and very climactic in nature. If we could, by our imagination, project ourselves back to the time of the Levitical system, we would recognize that the only way out of our sin was to take one of our own animals and after bringing it to the priest lay our hands upon its head and confess all our sins before the priest. Then we would watch him slit the jugular vein of the animal so that the life could spurt out into a basin to be sprinkled upon us and poured before the altar. Furthermore, we would watch the death, which was rightfully ours, take control of the animal, while the life that belonged to the animal was vicariously sprinkled on us. We would have to admit that it was an almost traumatic experience. It wasn't as easy as joining a church or writing a check for our tithe. We were involved! It was a crisis confrontation of sorts.

And yet this experience had to be repeated endlessly, because it was not a continuing experience, for not until Christ Jesus died as God's Lamb was there any continuing experience of the cleansing from sin.

So we do need the decisive crisis experiences, the brief moments of divine intervention into our affairs. None would ever want to fault the person who says: "It was in the spring of 1924 that the Lord graciously saved me," or "It was in September 1931 that I was gloriously filled with the Spirit," or "It was March 1975 that I was so wonderfully healed." All of these eventful experiences are necessary. They are proper and preparatory and, therefore, enable us to ascend out of ourselves, our sicknesses, or our sins into the presence of God for a short, momentary confrontation with God that is both life changing and mind boggling. May God give all of us more of them!

But the basic reason for these experiences is that until we see, we will not seek. All who have experienced leadership responsibilities have discovered that until they can sell a vision, they can never get people involved in a program. Until people *see* the things of God, they will never seek the things of God. "Where there is no vision, the people perish . . ." (Proverbs 29:18). The Berkeley Bible translates this: "Where there is no vision the people run wild. . . ."

While the Bible does declare: "For we walk by faith, not by sight" (2 Corinthians 5:7), we require sight of something before faith can begin to function. God must, first of all, give us the vision before we will arouse the inner vitality to move toward it. God first moves us to a mountaintop experience to give us an overall view of where we are going, then urges us down the other side through the marshland and across the desert toward this vision. This walk requires faith, but not blind faith. We've seen our destination from a distance. We know where we are headed because we have had a glimpse of it. Hebrews 11:13 affirms this in telling us: "These all died in faith, not having received the promises, but *having seen them afar off,* and were persuaded of them, and embraced them, and confessed that they were strangers and pilgrims on the earth" (italics added).

The initial crisis experiences may come without much sight for they are sovereign interventions of God, designed to initiate the novice into the supernaturals. They give glimpses into a realm that only a walk of faith can bring us into; yet those visions etch themselves into our memory in an unerasable manner.

But God does not want us to live totally in memories of past experiences. He doesn't want to have *done* something in our life, he wants to be *doing* something in it. Equally, God does not want us to live solely in hope, even the glorious hope of the Second Coming of Christ, which the Word declares is a great motivation for purification in the lives of the believers. It is a dangerous practice to merely live in hope when God has made it possible to live in relationship with His Son now.

There is something in the realm of continuous experience in God that He wants to bring His more mature saints into so that they don't just crisis out, drop off, and come into another crisis experience. God desires that the crisis experience will do its work to prepare us for and motivate us towards a continuum in God.

If we don't learn to break the crisis cycle, we are apt to find ourselves looking for gimmicks to lift us up once again. But the greatest "lift" God ever made available is His Lord Jesus Christ, whom He lifted up—first, on the cross, second, from the tomb, and finally, into the heavens. He then promised that we can be lifted up with and in Christ.

Dare we be content to have ascended when we find ourselves abiding in nearly the same manner of life we knew before our climactic experiences? David wanted to go beyond ascent; he wanted to know how to abide, to live in God's presence. "LORD, who shall abide in thy tabernacle? who shall dwell in thy holy hill?"

The remaining verses of Psalm 15 list five adjustments in our Christian behavior that are necessary in order for us to enter into an abiding relationship with God. That is what this book is about. We'll look at these adjustable areas one by one, considering how we can make our walk, works, words, will, and wealth conform to God's pattern; so we may abide in God's presence.

The first thing God wants to adjust is our walk, not to cripple us as Jacob, but to free us from the crippling flesh as the man at the Bethesda pool to whom Jesus said: ". . . wilt thou be made whole? . . . rise . . . and walk" (John 5:6–8).

2

An Adjusted Walk
Aids Abiding

He that walketh uprightly. . . .

During my early years of ministry, I was as crippled spiritually as the man at the pool of Bethesda. I could get to the pool of supernatural intervention only if carried by another or on crutches. It seemed that I spent much of my time building or repairing those crutches. I insisted on having my sermon preparation completed by Thursday evening since Friday was a day to relax, but Saturday was the day to press myself into God's presence. I would read, pray, meditate, and earnestly try to feel and be spiritual. Often this would continue until late into the night, and occasionally it would last all night long. I was trying to get myself "high enough" to be able to minister effectively. On Sunday I would seek to maintain this high, usually even refusing to take a nap for fear I would lose the blessing of the Lord.

Often I succeeded in attaining real spiritual heights, but Mondays were miserable. I frequently felt like I had made the first descent on an oversized roller coaster. On Tuesday I would begin to level out, and by Friday evening I was again preparing to climb back into the glory of God. It was a definite roller-coaster ride for me both emotionally and spiritually. Often the disappointment of the rapid descent from the spiritual highs so overwhelmed and depressed me that I would wait a few weeks before attempting to press into God's presence again. It was work, hard work, and so short-lived as to be disappointing. I was desperately and deliberately applying the means of grace that qualified me for a crisis experience of God's presence, but I did not know that it was possible to live in intimate fellowship and relationship with God through "the communion of the Holy Ghost" (*see* 2 Corinthians 13:14). No one told me that the Spirit had been given to make radical changes in my behavior, only that He came to empower my service. But I discovered that empowered ministry, which is not the outgrowth of dynamic relationship, is a drain both on the emotions and the body.

Although the ministry seemed to succeed, I lived with a sense of personal failure. When functioning under the anointing, I was one person, but out from under the anointing, I was a different man. My confidence crumbled, and elation was followed by depression. Public success only made my personal failures more painful. I could empathize with Paul's cry: "O wretched man that I am! who shall deliver me from the body of this death?" (Romans 7:24). I had not been taught to *abide in Christ.* I had only been introduced to the roller coaster of emotional and short-term experiences.

One day Jesus asked me, "Wilt thou be made whole?"

As my self-pity cried itself into a submissive "Yes, Lord," He began to speak to me about my walk.

This consistently is the first adjustment He requires before we can abide in His presence. We'll not be carried in either by another (no matter how blessed the conference or how anointed the speaker) or by means (crutches of laying on of hands or prophesy). But like the children of Israel, who had to walk out of Egypt and through the wilderness before they could walk into Canaan, we will have to learn to walk *into and with God.* God could have supernaturally transported that entire nation into the Promised Land, but instead He elected to supernaturally lead them in their day-by-day, natural walk, and so He does with us.

Holy Ghost
1) makes radical changes in my behavior
2) empowers my service

Some things God does for us, other things He does with us. While Ephesians 2:8 says: "For by grace are ye saved through faith . . ." verse 10 adds: "For we are his workmanship, created in Christ Jesus *unto good works,* which God hath before ordained that we *should walk in them*" (italics added).

So it is not sufficient to have a changed background, for after this is effected by God's action, the believer's behavior must be changed by personal action.

Remember that Jesus ministered most graciously to vast multitudes in healing their sick, raising their dead, opening blind eyes, and blessing their children. On at least two occasions He fed several thousand people in the wilderness. But of those who had ascendancy experiences with Jesus, there were twelve who were chosen for something special—something even more specific than the seventy who had been sent out two by two with great power and deliverance ministries. "And he ordained twelve, that they should be with him . . ." (Mark 3:14). To these twelve men Jesus said something He did not say to others, except the rich young ruler, when He said: "Follow me" (*see* Matthew 4:19).

To follow the Lord meant that they had to forsake their fishnets, their tax collecting, and their normal pursuits in life and involve themselves in the life-style their new Master would teach. This created problems as real for them as it creates for us to follow Him.

It is so easy to exclaim: "Oh, I'd just love to live in His presence. Last night's service was like a foretaste of heaven; I'd give anything just to be able to live in an atmosphere like that."

You can, but you can't live in the fishing boat and walk with Jesus simultaneously. Our behavior and style of living are probably the greatest deterrents to entering into His behavior and style of living. It is because we are involved here that we're not involved there in God's presence. "Follow me" has always been Christ's highest call. Jesus said: "My sheep hear my voice . . . and they follow me" (John 10:27). The emphasis is not merely upon hearing Jesus but following Him after we have heard Him.

At least thirty-six times in the New Testament the believer's experience is called a walk. Before they were called "Christians" at Antioch, the early believers were called "those of the way" (*see* Acts 9:2). They were known by their walk. Their experience was not static; it was progressive.

I meet many people who claim to desire to be led of the Lord and are inertly awaiting guidance. But the first law of guidance is motion. It is impossible to guide a car until you get it moving. If you want a car that is parked headed east to go west, start driving it east and then guide it into a U-turn.

To follow the Lord we have to move out from where we are, because we have become inert, and we have to break the inertia with momentum before we can get guidance. So the Holy Spirit tells the believer thirty-six times: "Walk—walk—walk."

God wants us to get moving. Start walking! We've sat long enough; it is time to step. We've learned to emote; now it's time to locomote. We've been free with the talk; now it's time to walk.

But walking is so unglamorous. Have you ever seen the bumper sticker I'D RATHER BE FLYING? That expresses my spirit. I far prefer the Scripture which speaks of "mounting up with wings as eagles" (*see* Isaiah 40:31) to the one which says, "How ye ought to walk and to please God" (*see* I Thessalonians 4:1). I've enjoyed some of those soaring experiences, but oddly enough, I didn't find many soaring eagles who needed ministry. As glorious and exhilarating as soaring experiences are, most ministry and development occurs in the everyday walk of life.

For instance, do we remember the results of the great campaign the disciples set up for Christ in Jericho? Of course not. We have no record of it in the Word. But we do remember that in His walk to Jericho He met and healed blind Bartimaeus.

Do we even know where Jesus was headed when He stopped at the well in Sychar? But we do know the result of the "chance" encounter with the woman at the well.

On another occasion Jesus seemed headed through Jericho towards something important when He spotted a man in a tree. The conversation of Zacchaeus is known to most Sunday-school children.

Are not our most vital encounters in the home, the shop, the school, and on the job? We find people open to us in nonspiritual situations. While some people will be reached in the church, most will be reached where they are by contact with a Christian who reflects the love of God even when he is not in a high spiritual state.

How vital it becomes, then, for us to come into an abiding life relationship that will be reflected in our walk, for that's where we'll be representing God and His Kingdom. As I used to hear it quoted when I was a boy: "Your life speaks so loudly, I can't hear what you say."

When aged David was grooming young Solomon to be king over Israel, he charged him: "And keep the charge of the LORD thy God, *to walk in his ways,* to keep his statutes . . . that thou mayest prosper [Berkeley says succeed] in all that thou doest . . ." (1 Kings 2:3, italics added).

After his coronation, God appeared to Solomon in a dream and said in part: "And thou wilt *walk in my ways,* to keep my statutes and my commandments, as thy father David did walk, then I will lengthen thy days" (1 Kings 3:14, italics added).

Still later, during the construction of the temple, we read: "And the word of the LORD came to Solomon, saying, Concerning this house which thou art in building, if thou wilt *walk in my statutes,* and execute my judgments, and keep all my commandments to *walk in them;* then will I perform my word with thee, which I spake unto David thy father: And *I will dwell among* the children of Israel, and *will not forsake my people* Israel" (1 Kings 6:11–13, italics added).

To this teenage boy, saddled with the responsibilities of the kingdom so securely welded together by his forceful father, David, God pledged: (1) success, (2) lengthened days, (3) to dwell among them, and (4) never to forsake His people. But all of these promises were built on the condition: "If thou wilt walk in my ways."

The entire life span of succeeding kings of Israel is passed over in Scripture with the simple statement: "He walked not in the ways of the God of his fathers." (*see* 2 Kings 21:22).

It is not, therefore, simply our position, "kings and priests unto God" (*see* Revelation 1:6), but our disposition, our walk, that determines the relationship level we will have with God. As we walk obediently with Him in His revealed ways, we enjoy His success, eternal life, abiding presence, and security. He will never take these things away from us, any more than He will give them to us. He simply shares them with those who will walk with Him as Adam, Enoch, Noah, Abraham, and others did. When we insist upon walking in our own paths we automatically lose the benefits of walking in His ways. He doesn't withdraw anything from us; we walk away from the very source of supply.

As we read the Word can't we hear our Lord calling: "Israelites, walk out of your tents and into My courts. Kings, walk in My ways and share My wisdom and success. Disciples, walk out of your occupations and occupy yourselves with Me. Christians, walk out of your earthly citizenship and into heaven's citizenship. Believers, forsake your ways and embrace My ways."

Paul paraphrased this saying: Walk in newness of life" (*see* Romans 6:4). The New English Bible translates it "the new path of life."

As surely as the priest had to walk out of his tent, into and through the outer court, into and through the holy place, and then through the veil into the holy of holies to come into the presence of God, so we, too, must walk out of some of the normal, everyday, proper, sinless activities of life in order to deliberately set our pace to walk into His presence. Otherwise, we'll never know a place of abiding in His presence. Although He came to us in crisis experiences, we must now go to Him for the continuing experiences.

Walking just to be in motion may be good exercise, but it never gets you anywhere. No amount of walking will bring you to your destination unless you either know where you are going, or have someone to guide you. Therefore, to help guide us in walking out of that which hinders our living in the abiding presence and into that realm that leads us into His divine Kingdom, the New Testament gives us four ardent admonitions concerning our walk: Walk in the Spirit; Walk in faith; Walk in love; and Walk in the light. These seem to be the four major compass points for guiding our walk into the recognized presence of God.

Walk in the Spirit, Not in the Flesh

In Galatians 5 Paul calls for us to "Walk in the Spirit, and ye shall not fulfil the lust of the flesh" (*see* v. 16). Following this admonition Paul lists eighteen activities which he calls "the lust of the flesh," but which many today call demon activity. The list logically falls into four general categories.

Sins of misdirected physical desire are listed as "adultery, fornication, uncleanness, lasciviousness" (*see* v. 19).

Sins of misdirected faith are called "Idolatry, witchcraft, hatred" (*see* v. 20).

Sins of misdirected brotherly love are titled "variance, emulations, wrath, strife, seditions, heresies" (*see* v. 20).

Sins of excess are given as "Envyings [excessive desire to possess], murders [excessive anger], drunkenness [excessive imbibing], revellings [excessive pursuit of pleasure] and such like [any excessive pursuit of normal human drives] (*see* v. 21).

God's Word simply says that we can walk out of these things if we learn to walk in the Spirit. I do not mean to minimize the ministry of exorcism, for I know that giving ourselves over to the lusts of the flesh often opens a channel for demonic activity in us in these areas. And if one is actually demonized in any of these areas, he may well need deliverance. But if giving ourselves to the works of the flesh opens the door to demon activity against us, then

giving ourselves to the walk of the Spirit should close that door to
demon activity.

No amount of casting out of demons is going to close the door
to their activity. This has been the heartbreak of much of the
deliverance ministry of the past few years. The faith of another can
force the demons to flee, but only the action of the demonized
individual can keep them from returning with reinforcements (*see*
Matthew 12:45).

God says that the best way out of these works of the flesh and
the possible demonic activity that frequently accompanies them is
to walk in the Spirit. You cannot cast out the "works of the flesh"
even though you may successfully cast out any energizing influence
that may have attached itself to that work. Whatever energy of
redemption may have come to release us from the power of sin, it
takes a deliberate act of the believer to walk out of the presence of
sin. For each work of the flesh that has controlled us, we must
deliberately take a step into the Holy Spirit's path which guides us
into a new walk.

It is probably not an all-night prayer meeting that is needed to
get a person out of the works of the flesh, but an all-life walking
in the Spirit. It will be that day-to-day, hour-to-hour, and on some
occasions moment-to-moment obedience to prompting of the Spirit
to do what He says, to walk as He says, to obey His will instead
of our will that determines the difference between the person who
lives in the Spirit (*see* Galatians 5:25), and the person who lives
according to the dictates of his own flesh.

We are only out of the ways of the flesh as long as we are walking
in the ways of the Spirit, and it is possible for us to walk in the ways
of the Spirit part of the day and in the ways of the flesh part of the
day, thereby creating such a mixture as to confuse both ourselves
and those around us. So this passage urges us to get tuned to the
Spirit and walk in Him. We're not to just sing in the Spirit or shout
in the Spirit or merely worship in the Spirit but to *walk* in the
Spirit. Doing so will immunize us against walking in the lusts of

the flesh. It will not immunize us from having the lusts of the flesh, only from fulfilling them. We shouldn't censure ourselves or another when we find a lusting for something that is not of the Spirit's desire; we only judge ourselves if we submit to it. It is one thing to yearn for a watermelon, and quite another thing to steal one.

Remember that walking in the Spirit is never the forfeiting of the control of our life. It is simply receiving a new set of instructions. *Obeying*

I spent much of my boyhood days in Oregon and subsequently spent nearly fifteen years ministering in that beautiful state. Although its entire western border is the Pacific Ocean, producing beaches whose beauty is unexcelled in any place I have been in the world, its major seaport is Portland, which is nearly one hundred miles inland from the sea. The city is built at the convergence of the Willamette and the Columbia rivers, and all sea traffic comes from the ocean up the Columbia River to the port.

This has made the services of harbor pilots necessary. These men are specialists on the river channel. By prior arrangement the pilot meets the ocean vessel well beyond the river bar and is taken directly to the pilothouse of the ship. From the moment of his arrival, the safety of the vessel is in the hands of this specialist. He has spent his life on this river and knows every sandbar, shallow shoal, and treacherous current. He can guarantee safe passage from the ocean, across the bar, and up the winding course of the river to a safe docking in Portland. He is well respected, highly paid, and much sought after. During busy seasons ships will lie at anchor in the ocean awaiting their turn for this expert.

Yet this highly specialized navigator never touches the wheel of the ship and never issues an order to the engine room. He just stands behind the captain and states the proper action to be taken, leaving it up to the captain to issue the orders and to make the necessary correction in course. Although he is needed, he is not the captain of the ship. He never accepts the ultimate responsibility for the ship, only the responsibility to correctly inform the captain what to do. At any point the captain can refuse to follow his orders.

The harbor pilot has no power to enforce his instructions. The ultimate decision is the captain's, and the results of those decisions rest upon that captain.

Similarly, the Holy Spirit does not enter our life to take its control out of our hands. He never intends to become the captain. He enters at our request as a highly specialized guide through waters and courses well known to Him but totally new to us. He stands beside us in the control room of our life, our spirit, ("The Spirit itself beareth witness with our spirit . . ." [Romans 8:16]) and faithfully—but ever so gently—instructs us in the way we should go. The issuing of the commands in our life is left up to us. So walking in the Spirit is accepting the Spirit's guidance, His suggestions, and His instructions. He may speak ever so firmly, but He will never violate our command over our life through force.

All who have taken flight training know the difference between an automatic pilot and an instructor pilot. The automatic pilot is a very sophisticated electronic guidance device that, when properly tuned to navigational radio signals, fully takes over the flying of the airplane. The pilot need do nothing once everything is properly set. There are far too many stories of private pilots who have gone to sleep at the controls, so great was their trust in the automatic pilot.

All commercial airplanes are flown with such systems. A few years ago I was riding West in a 747 Jumbo Jet from New York. The approach and landing in San Francisco was extremely smooth, and the touchdown was perfect. After the plane had been slowed down to taxi speed, the pilot came on the intercom to tell us that the entire approach and landing had been done by a new form of automatic pilot and that he had not touched the controls of the plane for more than an hour.

In contrast to that, an instructor pilot is one who, although a highly qualified pilot in his own right, sits alongside the student consistently giving instructions to him so that the student can fly the plane. In the early period of instruction he may talk almost continuously, often having to give the same instruction repeatedly, but only in dire danger does he take over the controls himself. His purpose is to teach another to fly, not to fly the plane for him.

The Holy Spirit will never be an automatic pilot for our lives. At no time can we completely take our hands off the controls and say, "I give my life completely to You; You run it," even though that would be a very pleasant cop-out from responsibility. God has made no provision to turn redeemed men into robots whose lives are controlled by an outside influence. He came to free men from such demonic control. Christ paid too great a price in restoring our free moral agency to violate it now in the guidance center of our being.

Far from being our automatic pilot, the Holy Spirit comes to be an instructor pilot. He is called by Jesus a "paraclete" or "one called alongside to help." (*see* John 14:16. The Greek *parakletos* means "comforter.") He knows how to do, will tell us how to do, and will actually risk His own safety living within us while we learn to do, but He will not do it for us. Jesus said of the Spirit: "He dwelleth with you, and shall be in you" (*see* John 14:17), and "He will guide you into all truth. . . . he shall receive of mine, and shall shew it unto you" (*see* John 16:13, 14).

Since God is totally Spirit without flesh or soul, we must fellowship Him in the spirit realm of our tripartite nature. Only as we learn to live by divine rules in the realm of our spirit is there opportunity for us to enjoy intimate and continual fellowship and communion with God. "Walk in the Spirit," "Live in the Spirit," and "Be led of the Spirit" are the cries of Paul in Galatians 5.

Walk in Faith, Not in Fear

Walking by faith is more than a command; it is a condition without which "it is impossible to please him [God]" (*see* Hebrews 11:6). For this reason no theme in Scripture is more fully developed than the theme of walking by faith. Faith is mentioned well over three hundred times in the New Testament. Hebrews II is a hall of fame for great heroes and heroines of faith. It lists seventeen individuals by name plus refers to "elders, women, and others who "obtained a good report through faith" (*see* vv. 2, 39). Not only does it list these giants of faith, but it describes more than thirty great, impossible, undoable acts they accomplished through divine faith. It is an inspiring chapter to read when personal faith seems to ebb.

The great truth revealed to the dismayed Prophet Habakkuk— "The just shall live by his faith" (*see* 2:4)—is quoted three times in the New Testament (*see* Romans 1:17; Galatians 3:11; Hebrews 10:38) and became the rally cry for the Reformation under Martin Luther. Paul had seen the truth many years before when he declared, "I live by the faith of the Son of God, who loved me, and gave himself for me" (*see* Galatians 2:20).

The life of faith is not optional; it is obligatory. It was never offered as an elective for the supersaints. It is not a matter of preference; it is a prerequisite to divine life. Therefore, great portions of the Old Testament are devoted to revealing, often in painstaking detail, the steps God used to develop a life and walk of faith in His men. Inasmuch as we are told: "Whatsoever is not of faith is sin" (*see* Romans 14:23), we can understand why so much space is given in the Scriptures to unfold this theme.

But it is in the epistles of the New Testament that we find the inventory of the rewards of faith, for there we find at least sixteen areas of divine grace available to us through faith. For faith is listed as the source of, or channel for our: access to grace, healing, indwelling of Christ, justification, life, promise of the Spirit, propitiation, protection (shield and breastplate), righteousness, salvation, sanctification, standing, strength, steadfastness, understanding, and walk. A good concordance will list multiple references for each of these themes.

Volumes have been written on faith, and as long as each man must learn the pathway of faith for himself, we can be assured that more books will be written on it. But the Bible does not seek so much to define it as to direct it. The only concise definition of faith given us in the Scriptures is in Hebrews 11:1: "Now faith is the substance of things hoped for, the evidence of things not seen."

This short verse tells of five fundamental factors faceted in faith. The first is that *faith operates in the present. "Now* faith is. . . ." God has given us hope for the future and loving memories for the past, but faith is a force that operates in the here and now. Faith is not *going to do*—faith *does!*

In the story of the raising of Lazarus (John 11), Martha was the first to meet Jesus upon His arrival. Her greeting was, "Lord, if thou hadst been here, my brother had not died" (*see* v. 21). She attempted to express faith for the past.

Jesus answered, "Thy brother shall rise again" (*see* v. 23).

"I know that he shall rise again in the resurrection at the last day" (*see* v. 24), Martha responded, trying now to release faith in the future.

But Jesus demanded an action of faith in the present in saying, "Said I not unto thee, that, if thou wouldest believe, thou shouldest see the glory of God?" (*see* v. 40).

How much time is wasted and how many victories lost by mis-understanding memory of the past and hope of the future and placing them before faith. Anyone can believe for a past event, and it is not too challenging to believe for a future action, but to release divine faith in the present here and now is quite another thing. Faith functions in the now! Our walk in God is in the here and now. God is not locked into our time and space confines. He is in eternity which is a great eternal *now.* God has no past and no future. "Jesus Christ the same yesterday, and to day, and for ever" (Hebrews 13:8).

The second facet of faith reflected in this verse is in the simple statement: "Faith is. . ." Faith is not producible, but it is receivable. Faith is an energy as real to the divine world as electricity is real to the human world. It is produced in God, "Have faith in

God" (*see* Mark 11:22), and is transmitted when He speaks, "So then faith cometh by hearing, and hearing by the word of God" (Romans 10:17). This faith is released when we speak to the problem saying what God said to us in His Spirit: "Whosoever shall say unto this mountain, Be thou removed, and be thou cast into the sea; and shall not doubt in his heart, but shall believe that those things which he saith shall come to pass; he shall have whatsoever he saith" (*see* Mark 11:23). There is absolutely nothing we can do to manufacture faith; we can only receive it and release it. Faith is inherent in God's nature. When He speaks, He totally believes what He says will come to pass, and we receive not only the spoken word but the absolute confidence with which it was spoken. And, therefore, we have the courage to speak His Word to the situation. It comes to pass not because of our confidence but because it is His Word being spoken through human instrumentality.

My parents had five children—four boys and a girl. Mother was an absolute authoritarian. All of the children were required to be at the table when the meal was served. Often the boys would be playing ball away from the house as mealtime approached, and our little sister would be sent with the dinner call. She would come to the play area and cry, "Boys, dinner's ready. Come home." Usually she would be completely ignored, especially if the play was interesting at the moment. Stamping her little foot, she would repeat her urgent message, only to be ignored further. She would often return home in tears to inform Mother that the boys wouldn't listen to her. Mother would listen to her story of rejection and then tell her to return saying, *"Mother* said, dinner is ready." When that tiny, preschool, girlish voice thundered with great authority, *"Mother said* . . . ," the game was stopped immediately. We knew we were no longer dealing with our baby sister but with Mother.

Just so, when saints speak what they have heard God say, no matter how young, timid, or ineffectual they are, something happens in response to their cry, *"God said. . . ."*

The Christian does not produce the faith any more than my

sister did. We simply receive it when God speaks to us. Faith is "obtained" (*see* 2 Peter 1:1; Hebrews 11:2, 39); it is God given (*see* Romans 12:3). We dare not allow ourselves to say: "There is no faith in this situation." We must be honest enough to admit that we're simply not receiving His faith in this situation. Faith *is* whether we are receiving it or not.

A third factor of faith defined in Hebrews 11:1 is, "Now faith is the *substance*. . . ." The Greek word used here is *substratum* meaning "what stands under." Our English word suggests the same connotation. *Stance* is "a way of standing" and *sub* is a prefix meaning "under." Faith is what stands under a man or that upon which the man stands. To walk with God we cannot always stand on facts and can rarely trust feelings, but we can always stand firmly upon unshakable faith. If God said it, nothing can sway it. God's precepts always contain God's power. In our present changing world, when it seems that everything that can be shaken is being shaken, it is marvelously reassuring to have divine faith to stand upon. It has stood the test of time, and thousands before us have found it an immovable foundation upon which to build their lives.

The fourth fundamental of faith mentioned in this verse is faith's relationship to hope. "Faith is the substance of things *hoped for*. . . ." The New English Bible translates Colossians 1:4–6: ". . . we have heard of the *faith* you hold in Christ Jesus, and the *love* you bear towards all God's people. *Both spring from the hope* stored up for you in heaven—that hope of which you learned when the message of the true Gospel first came to you" (italics added). Hope, which springs eternal under God, feeds both our faith and our love. It is the wellspring from which faith and love flow.

This is especially meaningful in light of the verse which speaks of "Christ in you, the hope of glory" (*see* Colossians 1:27). If Christ Jesus our Lord is the true hope God has imparted to the church, then our faith should be constantly strengthened: by Christ in us, by His Spirit, Christ unto us, in His Word, and Christ for us, in the heavens as an interceeding High Priest. How surely, then, does He become the "author and finisher of our faith" (*see* Hebrews 12:2). This helps us to better understand why Paul finished his beautiful soliloquy on love with the motto: "Now abideth faith, hope, and love, and the greatest of these is love" (*see* 1 Corinthians 13:13). All three will endure eternally, for hope feeds faith on the one hand and love on the other. Therefore, the man who has learned to walk in faith will never be without hope or love.

Still a fifth truth about faith, as given in Hebrews 11:1, is that "Faith is the . . . *evidence* of things not seen." Faith is basically the believing of the word of another and accepting the unseen as real; then faith also moves into that unseen making it become a fact. Faith is believing the unseen; the reward of faith is seeing what we believed. That which faith has seen and touched becomes as real to the believer as that which his natural eyes have seen and his human hands have handled.

So many draw away from accepting anything by faith saying that it is neither rational nor scientific. Yet most major scientific breakthroughs started as an unproved premise that someone believed in enough to act on. Long before they could prove it in a test tube, or by a computer, they saw it by faith. In the spiritual world God declares an actuality that doesn't harmonize with facts, as we know them, in our human world. And faith lays hold upon God's declaration not because it understands it but because it has reason to believe the speaker, God. In reaching into the unseen world through faith, the reality of what God said becomes demonstrable.

Abraham and Sarah had to embrace the promise of a son by faith. But that faith reached into God's divine world and brought forth a son that everyone could see. Isaac became faith's first line of evidence to the household of Abraham. Faith reaches into the realm of the intangibles, lays hold of God's promises, and produces tangible evidence for others to see. It is understandable, then, that it is called a *"precious* faith" (*see* 2 Peter 1:1) and *"holy* faith" (*see* Jude 20, italics added). Its value is priceless, and its virtue is peerless.

Since no one can dwell in God's holy hill without developing a walk of faith, we must adjust from our past training of walking by facts to walking by faith—from understanding to believing. We need to turn from the control of our trained senses to the control of His trusted voice. How else could we ever have consistent communion with God?

But such a walk of faith will have its enemies. Probably the greatest opposition to faith is fear. Unbelief, considered by some to be faith's greatest enemy, is simply the absence of faith. Fear is faith moving in the wrong direction. It is a confidence in the opposite of what God has spoken. In the realm of the demonic, fear is to demons what faith is to God—a commitment of your belief in their power. That is why demons consistently seek to produce terror; it causes men to fear them, which gives demons greater authority and ability in men's lives and affairs. Fear is tacit permission for them to function.

Because faith is so vital to our entering into a continual relationship with God, we can expect fear to be ever present. Somehow we innately fear the unknown. Almost every time an angel appeared to a person in the New Testament, the angel's first words had to be "Fear not." The sight of a creature from God's Kingdom produced fear, not faith. Jesus even had to calm the fear of His disciples after performing the miracle of the prodigious catch of fish (*see* Luke 5:10). It seems that no matter what level our faith may have attained, when we are confronted by anything beyond that level our initial response is fear. What is meant to produce faith within us is channeled into an opposite direction, and becomes fear.

Yet the Word assures us that "God hath not given us the spirit of fear; but of power, and of love, and of a sound mind" (2 Timothy 1:7). I am distressed, as I cross the length and breadth of our nation, to find such a high incidence of fear projection, all in the name of the Lord. Prophecies of doom and destruction have caused many saints to sell their homes and move into new territory, often into areas where there also had been prophecies of destruction. Others are proclaiming a coming famine of such magnitude that few will escape. The fear with which this has been received has caused many Christians to hoard canned goods, purchase dehydrated foods, convert maximum amounts of cash into gold, and, in general, prepare to forestall what they felt was a word from the Lord.

Now I don't care to argue the validity of these prophecies. I was not present when they were given, and it is hard to judge a prophecy, except by Scripture, especially if it is received thirdhand. But I am distressed that the response of the hearers has been one of faithless fear instead of fearless faith.

Last year God spoke very clearly to my wife and me to purchase a small, very old house in Tabb, Virginia. It required a vast amount of rebuilding, but it is in a beautiful location and serves our needs very well. I was amazed when people drove all the way from New York to express great surprise that I would purchase property in an area that God had prophesied would be destroyed by a tidal wave. They felt constrained to inform me of this and wondered if I could back out of the purchase. They found it hard to believe that the Lord would instruct me to purchase land there. When I insisted that I had acted on what seemed to be a confirmed word from God, they wondered what I would do when God fulfilled "His Word." I told them that either I will be away in conference ministry when the wave strikes, or I will drown. And either way will be all right with me. I don't intend to stay here forever anyway. Why should I act in fear after having acted in faith? Having purchased at His command, should I flee at the prospect of impending destruction?

Of what value will we be either to God or to the world if we all flee to the hills of Kentucky (as some from my area did) or to any "safe place" awaiting doomsday? Let's occupy until He comes! Even if these words of doom should prove to be accurate, why live in a present fear awaiting some coming judgment of God? Hasn't He always made ample provision for His children in the day of judgment? Doesn't Psalm 91 divinely affirm: "Thou shalt not be afraid for the terror by night; nor for the arrow that flieth by day; Nor for the pestilence that walketh in darkness; nor for the destruction that wasteth at noonday . . . Because thou hast made the LORD, which is my refuge, even the most High, thy habitation; There shall no evil befall thee, neither shall any plague come nigh thy dwelling (*see* vv. 5–10)." God does not give us a forewarning of coming events to produce fear, but to generate faith. Jesus told His disciples: "Now I tell you before it come, that, when it is come to pass, ye may believe . . ." (John 13:19). If we respond fearfully to every foretelling He may send, He will have to stop speaking to us.

David said, "What time I am afraid, I will trust in thee" (Psalms 56:3), but I prefer Isaiah's faith level: "I will trust, and not be afraid" (*see* Isaiah 12:2).

The man who walks in faith cannot walk in fear, for fear is faith going in the opposite direction. *But,* they say, *look at Noah. He prepared to ward off God's judgment.* No he didn't. He responded in faith to God's command to build an ark which later became the means of God's delivering him from the worldwide judgment. Everything Noah did was faith motivated. There is no record of fear reaction.

I was teamed in ministry with W. J. Ern Baxter this year at a C.F.O. (Camp Farthest Out) in Alma, Michigan, where he quoted this brief poem which pretty well sums up this matter of fearing the future.

> The worried cow would have last till now
>   If she hadn't run out of breath;
> But she feared her hay wouldn't last all day,
>   So she mooed herself to death.

We need not spend our time and resources trying to avert potential judgment, we need to involve our energies in a walk of faith. We need to get our eyes off what God may do to the wicked and fix them upon what He is doing for the righteous. We need not fear tasting God's judgment if we have enjoyed tasting His goodness.

Our favored Psalm 23, memorized by all who have a Sunday-school heritage, tells us, "Surely goodness and mercy shall follow me all the days of my life: and I will dwell in the house of the LORD for ever" (v. 6).

The man who is to "dwell in the house of the Lord for ever" must learn a walk of fearless faith, for he will consistently be dealing with the unknown and with one whose ways and thoughts are as far above ours as the heavens are above the earth (*see* Isaiah 55:8, 9).

Walk in Love, Not in Lust

Still a third exhortation given to us in the New Testament concerning our walk is *"Walk in love,* as Christ also hath loved us" (*see* Ephesians 5:2, italics added).

Faith without love is like bacon without eggs or bread without butter. We always think of them as paired. At least ten times in the Kings James translation of the New Testament, and even more times in some of the more modern translations, we see faith and love paired in the same Bible verse. Paul expresses the prime purpose of this pairing in saying, "Faith which worketh by love" (*see* Galatians 5:6). It takes love to get our faith working. It was God's love for us that brought us into a place of receptivity where we could hear God speak words of faith to us. It is that same love rebounding back to Him that motivates us to release His faith in our everyday world of activity.

Love not only gets our faith working for us, it gets and keeps it headed in the right direction. When we no longer believe God but begin to believe in our problems and the opposition, faith flows as fear. Try as we will, it is hard to conquer fear. It seems that the more we deal with it, the larger and stronger it becomes. God's antidote to fear is: "There is no fear in love; but *perfect love casteth out fear:* because fear hath torment . . ." (1 John 4:18, italics added).

God doesn't suggest that we try to conquer our fear with a frontal assault but that we simply spend some time flowing in "perfect love," and only Jesus can begin the flow of perfect love.

When my daughters were of grade-school age, I was pastoring a church in Yakima, Washington. The parsonage had a master bedroom downstairs, and two bedrooms upstairs where the girls slept. Often during the heat of the summer we would have severe lightning and thunderstorms in the middle of the night. Generally the first clap of loud thunder was followed by the sound of three pairs of little feet coming down the stairway in rapid succession, and three little girls would climb in bed between their mother and father without invitation. Often without a word being spoken, they would snuggle down and go back to sleep, while my wife and I stared at the ceiling alarmed at the closeness of the storm.

Now that they are married, and mothers in their own right, I have asked them whatever made them think we could protect them from the storm. Our daughters said that it never occurred to them that we couldn't and that if they could just touch us and feel the security of our love, they lost all fear.

When the storms of life are raging, and fear is billowing up in our spirit like a cumulus cloud, we can just flee to the perfect love of Jesus, reach out, and touch Him. His love will reverse the flow from fear to faith. Without directly dealing with our fear, faith will be renewed as we rest comfortably in His love. We are well assured, "For God hath not given us the spirit of fear; but of power, and of love, and of a sound mind" (2 Timothy 1:7).

One of the very few defining terms given in the New Testament for God is "God is love" (*see* 1 John 4:16). Love is part of the essential nature of God. Man cannot originate true love any more than he can originate real faith. Even our love for God did not originate with us, it is a reciprocal response. "Herein is love, not that we loved God, but that he loved us, and sent his Son to be the propitiation for our sins" (1 John 4:10). When we were exposed to the love of God, it flowed into us, through us, and back to God.

The first fruit that ripens after the Spirit comes is love. It cannot be otherwise for that is part of His very nature. We cannot hope to have continuing relationship with God without walking the walk of love. Since the Holy Spirit has been sent to make us "conformed to the image of his son" (*see* Romans 8:29) and since God's Son came as a divine expression of God's love (*see* 1 John 4:10), we can expect that one of the early adjustments in our walk must be out of lust into love.

Most of our life is lived in lust levels. Our Western society has built its merchandising around creating such a strong desire for a product that we will purchase it. Salesmen don't sell the steak; they sell the sizzle. And so much of our interpersonal relationships are based far more on lust than love. We respond to desires, become slaves to our lusts, and live in a society that seems to be saying, "If it feels good, do it."

But God has not called us to lust, He has called us out of lust into His love. Love is not a feeling, it is a commitment that often produces feeling, but functions faithfully with or without the sensation. Love is not simply concerned with getting; it is interested in giving. Love's first question is never, "What's in it for me?" for love is basically selfless. We need to reread 1 Corinthians 13 regularly and remind ourselves of some of the great qualities of love listed in this beautiful passage. None of these great characteristics are to be found in lust. Love's source is the very nature of God; so we will never fall in love, but we will rise to love.

Inasmuch as love is not simply an emotion of elation or ecstasy but a sharing of the nature of God, it will have both an origin (God) and an object to which it can be expressed. Unexpressed, love ceases to be a flowing river and often becomes a stagnant pond. While God is the only source for love, He is only one of several objects of our love. We are clearly taught in the New Testament to have at least three additional areas where love can flow unrestrictedly: the home, the brotherhood, and the neighborhood.

God has always been vitally interested in the home. It is the beginning unit of His church. It is a constant illustration in the naturals of the relationship He desires with us in His spiritual Kingdom—bride and bridegroom, husband and wife. It is significant that in the ten major Bible divisions (Pentateuch, Historic Books, Poetic Books, Major Prophets, Minor Prophets, Gospels, Acts, Pauline Epistles, General Epistles, and Revelation) our relationship with God is referred to as a marriage relationship. On earth He desires that "They two shall be one flesh" (*see* Ephesians 5:31), and in His relationship with us in His heavenly Kingdom He desires that we become one in Christ (*see* John 17:21).

This love relationship must be a spiritual relationship because God is incapable of lust. Ephesians 3:17–19 says: "That Christ may dwell in your hearts by faith; that ye. . . . May be able. . . . to know the love of Christ . . . that ye might be filled with all the fulness of God." It is expected, then, that the natural relationship, which is a type of the Divine, must also flow in love.

Four times in the New Testament husbands are commanded to "love your wife." The nature of the love required is very explicit. "Husbands, love your wives, even as Christ also loved the church, and gave himself for it" (Ephesians 5:25). "So ought men to love their wives as their own bodies. He that loveth his wife loveth himself" (v. 28). "Let every one of you . . . so love his wife even as himself" (*see* v. 33). "Husbands, love your wives, and be not bitter against them" (Colossians 3:19). To further strengthen this command these passages use the strongest Greek word for love— *agape*.

The Greeks use four separate words to convey various levels of love, while the English language uses one word for all levels, and often we even interchange *love* for *like*. The first Greek word for love, on an ascending scale, is *eros* from which we get our word *erotic*. The word never appears in the Scriptures. It is sort of a "strawberry-shortcake love" or that which satisfies passion. In its strongest sense it could be translated *lust*.

The second word is *storgay*. It is a phony love, sort of a popular-aunt love: "I have to love her because she is my aunt." It perhaps describes some of the love expressed to one another in our religious gatherings: "I have to love you to get to heaven."

The third word is *phileo*, which is sort of a baseball-team love: "If you're on my team, I'll love you." It has sometimes been translated "fond of."

But the highest Greek word for love is the word used here for husbands to "love their wives." It is *agape*, a self-giving love, a love of devotion.

The fact that a husband finds sexual satisfaction with his wife may not prove that he loves her in the manner the Bible commands. It may be little more than eros. She may be his strawberry short-cake, and he loves tasting it. But the Word calls for agape, a love that devotes itself, that gives itself, that puts the object of the love on an equal plane with himself.

Interestingly enough, the closest thing to a command given to the wife to love her husband is in Titus where Paul tells the aged women to "teach the young women to be sober, to love their husbands, to love their children" (*see* 2:4). They are not commanded to love their husbands, but it is suggested that they be taught to do so. The Greek word used here is not the same as the one used for the husband. Here it is *phileo*, the baseball-team sort of love or fond of. Wives are told to join the team of husband and children with at least a good team spirit.

By not requiring the wife to have the agape for her husband, the divine type is fulfilled. Love originates in God, the husband, and is given to us, the wife. We receive and respond to a love that originates in Him. Similarly, in the home, love should originate in the husband. It is he that should give himself for his wife and family. He, under God, can rise to agape love. When he projects this to his wife, she receives it, responds to it, and returns it back to her husband. Women are not only built to be receivers of true love, most of them also amplify it so that a little agape received is amplified sufficiently to meet the needs of husband, family, brother-hood, and neighborhood. While she may not be designed to origi-nate the love, she is intricately designed to receive it and return it greatly increased.

Many times I have counseled a husband to bring at least one kilowatt of love into his home, warning him that by the time his wife ran it through her amplifier, she would broadcast 100 mega-watts of love back to him.

Blessed is the home that functions with the flow of God's love. If it can't be shared there, it can't be shared elsewhere. There must be great security in love on this level before we dare share true love in the other two levels. We never dare substitute loving the brother-hood for loving the partner and children in our own home; it will only widen the breach that destroys the home.

But for one who is making an adjustment in his walk in love, a proper flow of agape love in the home is never sufficient. We are repeatedly commanded to release to the brotherhood the flow of this same level of love, which is the nature of love that flows from God to us.

Interestingly enough, John tells us to "love one another" nearly a dozen times in his brief writings. Brother Paul speaks repeatedly of "brotherly love," and more than thirty-five times uses the term *one another*. In 1 John 4 this theme is strongly stated: "Beloved, let us love one another: for love is of God; and every one that loveth is born of God, and knoweth God" (v. 7). "Beloved, if God so loved us, we ought also to love one another" (v. 11). "If a man say, I love God, and hateth his brother, he is a liar: for he that loveth not his brother whom he hath seen, how can he love God whom he hath not seen?" (v. 20). "And this commandment have we from him, That he who loveth God love his brother also" (v. 21).

This is not a call to a team spirit (phileo), so common in strong denominational settings, but in every one of these verses the Greek word for love is agape—devoted, divine love. This calls for more than a mere handshake on Sunday morning. It is a call for commitment, for sharing, for belonging to one another.

When, through circumstances beyond my control, I found my-self having to give leadership to a brand-new church in the New-port News area of Virginia, I first of all established an eldership for a plurality of leadership. I told them that if we were going ahead with this little group of people whose leader had been snatched away from them, through no fault of their own, we should produce something that seemed to be lacking in the other churches on the Peninsula—a true family spirit. It took some doing, but little by little we taught our people to express genuine love to one another. We started by substituting a hug for the standard handshake. We can shake hands with an enemy but can only hug a brother or sister. There was a sense of awkwardness at first, but as we adjusted to the unusualness of it, many emotional healings began to occur. More is communicated in a touch than in a lecture, if the subject is "I love you."

Then we began to bring our lunch with us every other Sunday, to stay for some fellowship around the tables, and to spend much of the afternoon together talking, singing, and praying with one another in a totally unstructured manner.

Something began to happen. Our "church" began to become a "family." Our concern of one for another reached beyond the walls of our worship center. Brothers became interested in the needs of the unmarried, widows, divorced, and service wives whose hus-bands were away on duty. Roofs were repaired, air conditioners fixed, cars serviced, and plumbing unstopped without the necessity of organization on our part. As soon as a need was known, a brother or two would accept the responsibility to see that the need was met.

Visitors are aware of something different in the atmosphere in the congregation. We've heard them say that they have received more love in one service with us than they had experienced in several years.

Should this be unusual or the norm? Is the true purpose of our fellowship to contact God and to love Him? Do we yearn to reassure ourselves that God dwells in us? The Word tells us: "If we love one another, God dwelleth in us, and his love is perfected in us" (*see* 1 John 4:12). Praise is not the only way to enter into the presence of God; loving the brethren is another.

A third area in which we are asked to walk in love is in relationship to the neighborhood. Eight times in the New Testament the command of Leviticus is quoted: "Thou shalt love they neighbour as thyself" (*see* 19:18). It is not love of our fellow churchmen, they are the brotherhood, but love our neighbor, those outside the fellowship of the church. In His parable of the good Samaritan, Christ established that our responsibility of loving one another must transcend race, creed, culture, and religious affiliation. They are not merely to be tolerated but to be loved as we love ourselves.

Once again the word for divine love is used. We may not find a social affiliation with them and may not sense being on the same team, but we can manifest divine love in all of our dealings with them. We can show genuine concern in time of their sorrow and assistance in time of their need, as well as share with them in times of their rejoicings.

Perhaps a major reason many have been hesitant to establish a love communication with their neighbors is a fear that something of their neighbor's ungodliness might rub off on them. But if we are infected with divine agape, we are carriers not catchers. We will infect them, not be infected by them. "Greater is he that is in you, than he that is in the world" (*see* 1 John 4:4). We really do not need to be in the isolation ward of the church, for the blood of Jesus Christ has immunized us against the contamination in the lives of the unbelievers. We may be in the world, but we are not of the world. Jesus prayed to the Father in His great high-priestly prayer: "I pray not that thou shouldest take them out of the world, but that thou shouldest keep them from the evil. . . . As thou hast sent me into the world, even so have I also sent them into the world" (John 17:15–18). Christ never cloistered His disciples away from mankind;

He sent them right into the mainstream of life.

If our love can extend beyond our personal homes into the church and on into the world, we will reach men and women for the Kingdom. Love is the only force that will draw them. They cannot see, feel, or understand the Kingdom of God, but they can respond to the love of God through you and me. We need not hoard the love, for its supply is inexhaustible; we are only its channel. We need never fear being cheated in giving love to the unlovely, for it isn't our love we are giving, it is God's love, and He "commendeth his love toward us, in that, while we were yet sinners, Christ died for us" (*see* Romans 5:8). The only thing it can cost us to love our neighbor is some time, and since our rebirth, we have already become creatures of eternity; so a little time lost here is of no consequence.

The fact that our neighbor is mentioned about 240 times in the Bible and that most of the references are concerned with our relationship to that neighbor should say something to us. The Word tells us we are not to covet anything our neighbor possesses or defraud him in any business dealings; never to get involved with him in any form of sexual impurity; not to bear false witness against him; not to rebuke him, or devise any evil against him. Conversely, we are simply to love him.

Probably the command to love our neighbor as ourself is more for our sake than the neighbor's. If we are directing the flow of the same agape love toward him that we are manifesting in the home and in the church, we will automatically exempt ourselves from any of the above prohibitions. Furthermore, if divine love, real Kingdom love, is flowing, there will be no room for our desiring or lusting after anything apart from His realm. We will see ourselves as rich in the goods of heaven's Kingdom and will not envy one who is merely rich in this earth's goods. Love, which is such an effective antidote for lust, is equally a potent inoculation against covetousness.

He who would abide in the heavenly realm must make an

adjustment in his walk of love, for "God is love; and he that dwelleth in love dwelleth in God" (*see* 1 John 4:16). We have to adjust to His nature in order to dwell in His presence. We'll be led of His Spirit, flow in His faith, live in His love, abide in His truth as well as walk in His light, for these are the essentials of God's nature.

Walk in Light, Not in Darkness

Therefore, since Jesus also said, "I am the light of the world" (*see* John 8:12), and it is recorded that "God is light, and in him is no darkness" (*see* 1 John 1:5), walking God's pathway will also compel us to adjust our way from darkness to light. We will have to abandon every dark way, every dark thing, and every practice of darkness. This is possible since Ephesians 5:8 declares, "For ye were sometimes darkness, but now are ye light in the Lord: walk as children of light." We may rest assured that nothing that smacks of darkness savors of the Lord. Light and darkness are an antithesis to each other. Where God is, there will be no darkness. His path will not even be shadowed with semidarkness. The communication on His path is not with the satanic world but with the divine world. The creatures of His habitation are not demons but angels. The future is not divined by horoscope but by the Holy Spirit. All of His works are works of light; there is nothing hidden or done in secret. What open-faced honesty this requires of believers! But this is His nature, and to know fellowship with Him, we will have to adjust to it.

But it is worth it, for He has promised, "If we walk in the light, as he is in the light, we have fellowship one with another" (*see* 1 John 1:7). This fellowship does not refer to relationships with other believers but to fellowship with the One with whom we have chosen to walk. It is Jesus and you in fellowship.

When Amos asked the question, "Can two walk together, except they be agreed?" (3:3), the answer is presupposed to be no. Obviously, we cannot walk with God unless we are taking the same pathway He is using. All of our prayers for God to walk with us are selfish and useless, for God's ways are unchangeable. If any adjustment in the pathway is to be made, we will have to do it. "I am the LORD, I change not" (*see* Malachi 3:6). We do not read in the Scriptures of God walking with man but of man walking with God. And so it shall ever be. In Revelation it is promised, "They shall walk *with me* in white" (*see* 3:4, italics added), while also mentioned is a group who "follow the Lamb whithersoever he goeth" (*see* 14:4). The mystery of a personal, intimate life in the presence of God is not solved by investigating the capricious choosings of God, but by looking at the adjusted walk of the believer who has found continuing fellowship with his God.

Hear the cadence of marching feet as the saints of the ages walk with God in righteousness—Noah in a walk of works, Moses on the path of obedience, Abraham on the route of faith, and David on the path of worship. They were joined by countless thousands of chosen ones who learned to adjust their walk into His righteous ways.

But who are these in the parade whose music is more saxophone and electric guitar than tabret and harp, who parade in cars instead of on camels, who are dressed in business suits rather than flowing robes? These are the men of today's generation who have stepped out from behind religious walls into a walk of vital relationship with their God. They've seen and heard something of the heavens and have set themselves in God's path of righteousness.

The way they take isn't new, but the marchers are. They are discovering the way of faith as though it had never been discovered before. They are exploring ancient footsteps in their search for the path of love. They are following a moving light lest they be caught again in darkness. They are the modern pioneers of the paths of an ancient God. They too will "walk with him in white." Their path of discovery has drastically affected their walk but soon will just as drastically change their works. But they are a rejoicing group ready to do what He says, when He says, and how He says, no matter what adjustments it requires of them.

3
Adjusted Works Aid Abiding

He that . . . worketh righteousness. . . .

If a man's walk has been changed, can his works remain unchanged? Does a collegian continue to function as he did in primary school? Of course not! Maturity, development, and growth automatically affect our behavior patterns.

Just so, the man who abides in God will produce works of righteousness as automatically as the abiding branch produces fruit in season. One is the outgrowth of the other.

"Who shall abide in thy tabernacle? . . . He that . . . worketh righteousness. . . ." (Psalms 15: 1,2).

Having embraced the means of grace through the cross and the Word sufficiently to have enjoyed momentary crisis experiences in God, he is now challenged to make this righteousness work for him and to get involved in the works of righteousness.

Even to the casual reader, this passage could not be interpreted to mean involvement in works produces righteousness, for there is nothing, absolutely nothing, we can do to produce righteousness. Not even leading souls to Christ or getting them filled with the Holy Spirit, not laying hands on the sick and seeing them recover, not playing the organ, singing solos, preaching sermons, or building buildings—*nothing we can do*—can produce righteousness. Nothing!

Organized religion almost universally functions on the premise: "A job for every man and every man in his job." It seems to feel a tremendous responsibility to get everyone working. Converts must be assigned a task even if it is only to water the flowers. "It will help them develop spiritually" is the argument. But working never makes us spiritual. Of course, if we are truly spiritual, we will indeed be working. But it is not the works that produce righteousness; it is the *right-wise-ness* (Old English) of our newfound relationship with God that produces the motivation to work.

Only God is righteous (*see* Romans 3:10), and unless He confers His righteousness, man remains not only unrighteous but without hope of righteousness.

Unfortunately, few men choose to believe this. They have set up elaborate rules, laws, systems, codes, and regulations, the observance of which is supposed to produce righteousness. But, alas, they never make a man righteous, only religious. There is no system of works, however much we may desire one, that can make us righteous in God's sight. Sin has so completely stripped us of righteousness that there doesn't even remain a small seed of righteousness to sprout into life no matter how tenderly we tend the soil.

But now that Christ, our righteousness (*see* 1 Corinthians 1:30), has taken residence within us through His Holy Spirit, we have been introduced into the divine Kingdom which is defined as "righteousness" (*see* Romans 14:17) and are encouraged to become "workers of righteousness" (*see* Psalms 15:2; Acts 10:35). While we cannot be producers of righteousness, we can be practitioners of it.

It is a matter of consummating in our living what has been conferred in God's giving. An embryo of righteousness has been imparted to us; now it is our responsibility to bring it to maturity in the inner womb of our love and to let it be brought forth as a living organism with both the name and nature of God upon it—true divine righteousness.

In Philippians we read: "Work out your own salvation with fear and trembling. For it is God which worketh in you both to will and to do of his good pleasure" (*see* 2:12, 13). Kenneth A. Wuest in his book *Golden Nuggets from the Greek New Testament* tells us that the Greek word translated here as "work out" carries the implication of working a problem in mathematics. That is, having been given the factors of the problem as well as the formula, do the necessary computation to arrive at a proper answer. Don't be content to know the rules of math or with simply having a correct equation; work out the problem to its ultimate conclusion.

God implanted the factors of His righteousness within us at the moment of our rebirth. He gave us the rules of computation in His Word. But it becomes incumbent upon us to work out the problem in the nitty-gritty of life. Where there needs to be multiplication, multiply ("Grace and peace be multiplied unto you" [*see* 2 Peter 1:2]). Where addition is called for, add ("Add to your faith . . . " [*see* 2 Peter 1:5]). Where subtraction is required, subtract ("But now ye also put off all these . . ." [*see* Colossians 3:8]). Even division is sometimes part of the process for working out divine righteousness, as seen in the scattering of the saints from the growing and powerful church in Jerusalem (*see* Acts 8:1–4), and in the division of Paul and Barnabas as coworkers with each taking a different partner and thus doubling the missionary ministry (*see* Acts 15: 39, 40). But we are to keep working on the problem until we get a solution.

I find quite the opposite view current in the thought life of many recent believers. They seem to manifest the threefold attitude: "If at first you don't succeed—*give up,* or *call up* someone to cast it out of you, or *show up* to have hands laid upon you." But Paul says for us to work out the solution.

When Paul was in Philippi, he helped the saints in their entrance into righteousness. He instructed, inspired, and encouraged them by his teaching, his exhortation, and his example. Later, confined to prison and helpless to assist them any further, he wrote them a reminder that they already possessed all the factors of righteousness through the goodness of God's grace, the giftings of the Spirit,

and the inner growth of the fruit of the Spirit. All that remained
to be done by them was to accurately and completely work out the
solution. What he had done for them in the past, they then had to
do for themselves. The early Christians were told to "build up
yourselves on your most holy faith" (*see* Jude 20). They were
charged to "teach and admonish one another in psalms and hymns
and spiritual songs . . ." (*see* Colossians 3:16). They were instructed
to "comfort one another with these words" (*see* 1 Thessalonians
4:18).

All that ever needs to be done to save us from sin and assure our
entrance into heaven has been done for us by Christ. But what
needs to be done to mature us from infancy to adulthood requires
much conscious work on our part. We will have to eat the Word,
rest in the Lord, exercise our faith, learn the ways of God, and be
willing to try and to fail over and over again until we have matured
in all areas of our life. Even Jesus did not escape this time-consum-
ing process, for we read, "And Jesus increased in wisdom and
stature, and in favour with God and man" (Luke 2:52).

None of us was born with knowledge, but each of us innately
possesses the ability to learn both naturally and spiritually. It is our
application of this ability that determines the level of knowledge
we will carry through life. Equally, it is not sufficient to have been
born righteous at our new birth; we must continuously apply ourselves to the development of this righteousness to higher and higher
levels. What we possess innately can be developed infinitely. The
world has never heard all who were born with an innate ability to
play the violin, for many spent their lives on farms, in factories, or
in diverse forms of business contenting themselves with occasional
fiddle playing to satisfy an inner craving. Only a few gave themselves seriously to the development of their gift. These are the
musicians the world has loved and remembered.

Similarly, the church has not seen all those with a lifelong call
serving the Lord. Too many of them never disciplined themselves
to develop this gift of God; they did not work it out. But volumes

have been written about some of those who gave themselves to fully consummate what God had conferred to them. Some have been revered as saints even in their lifetime. The difference is not in the inherent abilities but in what was done about these imparted gifts.

Two of the happiest times I enjoy in my role as a pastor are marrying young couples, and later dedicating their first child. Never will a man and woman radiate more happiness or exude such inner beauty as at these two moments. It is always a thrill to be a participant with them and to share in the flow of love each pledges to the other during the ceremony.

At the reception and during the early weeks following the ceremony, the lovely bride and groom declare to all listeners that theirs is a perfect blending; they are ideally mated. Theirs is an absolutely perfect marriage with no problems; they are superlatively suited to each other—"God did it."

Oh, boy, just wait a while! What God did was put in each the factors that meet the other's needs, but it will take years of working on it before their marriage becomes a perfect blend. My wife and I have spent thirty-three years, at the time of this writing, working on this problem called marriage and occasionally still find another factor in the formula that needs to be computed. The marriage is so much better than it used to be, and we thought it was good then. And it probably isn't as good as it is going to be, for we have not yet attained the ultimate. But it is marvelous.

The only hope for a marriage to succeed is to refuse to believe that the minister can mystically make you a husband and wife and to simply recognize that he can only give you a legal chance to try to become husband and wife. It will take a lot of doing, a lot of living, a lot of understanding, and a lot of working together to achieve that goal. There will be pain mixed with the pleasure, responsibilities accompanying the rejoicing, and misunderstandings balancing shared experiences. It must be worked at continually. It is never totally achieved.

As we've already seen, the entire Bible speaks of our relationship to God as a husband-wife relationship. God has introduced us, His bride, into a whole new realm of living that requires great adaptations to make it work. But since the Bible says, "Jesus Christ the same yesterday, and to day, and for ever" (Hebrews 13:8), if we're going to make this marriage to God work, we're going to have to do the changing; He doesn't change. Therefore, He gives us the factors of the problem, motivates us by His love for us, and says, "Work out the necessary changes." For all of His gifts and all of His desires do not produce the necessary changes in us. We must produce those changes; we must do the adjusting; we must let the righteousness of God work in us effectively. He gives an ample supply of righteousness and then leaves it to us to apply it.

To be among the saints who abide in God's tabernacle and to have a continuing relationship experience with Him, instead of crisis-related experiences, we must learn to "work righteousness," to let it mature, and also to let it involve us in works that are the outgrowth of our newfound relationship with God!

In 1 Corinthians 3 there are three levels of service, each progressively higher than the preceding one. In verses 5 and 6 Paul speaks of himself and Apollos as complementary ministers who had plowed, planted, and watered the fertile field in Corinth. He affirms that it was God who gave the increase. This graphically illustrates the first level of service we believers enter into whereby we do things *for* God. One man plows the field for God; another man plants it for God; and still a third waters it for God. They are His workmen, His laborers, His gardeners who work to produce the crop.

This is where we all start in our service for God. It is outer-court ministry, for everything done in the outer court of the tabernacle was done for God on God's behalf. It wasn't done by God but for Him by man.

All of this working *for* God tends to be a response to a precept. We see something in the Word and obediently respond to it. We read: "Go ye into all the world, and preach the gospel to every creature" (*see* Mark 16:15), and in response to it we become a missionary or at least develop a missionary vision. Or we read, "Ye shall be witnesses unto me" (*see* Acts 1:8) and begin passing out tracts everywhere we go. It is a matter of obediently responding to what we see in the Word. Much as the children of Israel who asked God to write down anything He wanted done and promised to do it, we tend to approach the Bible as a set of instructions for our service. This is not all bad. It teaches obedience, which is better than sacrifice (*see* 1 Samuel 15:22), and breaks the inertia of inactivity to set the stage for divine guidance into something better.

But working *for* God has two major weaknesses. First, it tends to be very need oriented. It is interesting to note that we rarely see the command in the Word until we have seen the need in man. We generally move from the need to the Word then back to the need. We are not, therefore, truly Word commanded; we are need commanded with Word authorization. Jesus, during His earthly ministry, refused to be need oriented. He was command controlled. He got His orders from the Father, not the people. He did what the Father desired, not what the multitudes demanded. He could say: "I delight to do thy will, O my God" (*see* Psalms 40:6–8; Hebrews 10:6–9).

Had Jesus been need oriented, He would never have gone to the pool of Bethesda to chose the one man the Father had selected to heal and then walk off, with the cripple restored to health after thirty-eight years of lameness, without healing anyone else. Surely this great multitude of people, awaiting the stirring of the water by an angel in anticipation that the first one into the pool would be healed, must have pleaded pitifully for a healing touch. But Jesus was not directed by need or compassion, He was directed by the voice of the Father. Jesus didn't always feed the multitudes; He didn't always heal the sick; He didn't always minister to all the obvious needs, because He was not need oriented. He did not come to alleviate human suffering; He came to reveal the Father. If meeting a need would reveal the Father, Jesus met that need. But whenever meeting the need would hinder revelation of the Father, He walked right on by. He said to His disciples, "For ye have the poor with you always . . ." (Mark 14:7), that is, you will always have needs around you.

Christ did not commission the disciples or us to destroy ourselves trying to meet all of the needs we see, but He has, in fact, commissioned us to reveal the Father to the world (*see* John 17:18). Oh, how many faithful ministers of the Gospel have been exhausted before their time just because they were need oriented, for it is but a tiny step from being need oriented to being need controlled. And whenever a man is controlled by the needs of others, he is automatically out of control. He finds himself on a never-ending treadmill, rushing from problem to problem and person to person and always administering emotional first aid but never having time to deal with the real sickness. Eventually it breaks him too, and the needy look for another they can control with their guilt-projecting problems.

Another weakness of merely working *for* God is that it often becomes very legalistic and harsh. Because these workers substantiate their ministry unto people through ample portions of the Bible, they tend to insist that everyone else do the same thing they do. They plead the universal authority of the Word and say that what is a command for them is a command for the entire Body of Christ. Any who would plead another form of ministry or claim to have received a direct command from the Spirit are generally branded as heretics and either disfellowshiped or regularly denounced. For one who cannot see beyond the needs around him there is no time available for ministering with God, and there certainly is no concept of ministering unto God. There usually is not sufficient grace operating within their lives to allow anyone else to see beyond their personal vision. They project that whatever is required of them is automatically required of all. It almost seems that the greater the misery in their level of ministry, the stronger their resentment of anyone who chooses another path of ministry.

They would make everyone plowmen or all men waterers or all must join them in sowing. They do not realize God's purpose in giving diverse ministries.

Many years ago, when I was pastoring in Yakima, Washington, my church had monthly services in the local Union Rescue Mission. The director, whom all affectionately called Brother Jimmy, had been saved from alcoholism in that very mission and was a great exponent of mission ministries. So great was his concern for the down-and-outers of that area that he tended to despise all other forms of ministry. He used to denounce the local churches and their pastors, all the while declaring that the ministry of the mission was a God-ordained ministry. Yet, he turned to the local churches for his support, for the nightly meetings, for staff assistance, and for special favors. It was not until the final few years of his ministry that he began to see that his calling was not necessarily *the* high calling of God for the body. It was simply *his* calling. It was an important calling but not the universal calling. His ministry continued to exist because many other ministries undergirded him and his mission and loaned their strength to him. It took years of maturing and the mellowing of age to remove this brother from the pedestal of harsh legalism.

Far too often those who begin by working *for* God get sidetracked into working for people in God's name and never know the difference. Their works are worthy; the needs seem honorable; and the dedication is harmonious with that of a martyr. They find ample Scripture portions to give validity to their ceaseless activity, which often must substitute for works of righteousness, and are deceived into believing that the substitute is the same as the substance. But social service and spiritual ministry can only be synonymous if it is done at the command of God.

Perhaps the popularity of this level of service is that it does not require an abiding relationship with God. It is something being done *for* God, not *with* Him. It is people centered and need oriented and tends to make us indebted to the beneficiaries.

The second level of Christian works is stated: "For we are la-bourers together with God" (*see* 1 Corinthians 3:9), or "Workers together with him" (*see* 2 Corinthians 6:1). Instead of merely work-ing *for* Him, we are invited to work *with* Him.

Assuming you have been a successful applicant for a job, would you prefer to hear on your first day of employment: "Here's a book of instructions, and there is the equipment. Follow the instructions, and you'll soon catch on," or: "Here, join me. You'll learn as we go along. I'll give you on-the-job training"—which? Assuming that the boss is a pleasant individual, certainly you would prefer to work *with* him than merely *for* him. No one knows better what needs to be done, when it should be done, or how to do it than the boss. All responsibility for decisions would be his, not yours. You would simply do what you were told, when you were told, as long as you were told, and feel no responsibility for anything you had not been told.

Why, then, do so many of us fear moving into the inner court to learn to minister *with* God? Why remain forever in the outer court with the open book, seeking instructions for our workings, when we have been invited into the inner court to learn to be "labourers together with God"?

To the Jews of His day, bound with rituals, rites, ceremonies, and ordinances of worship, Jesus said: "Come unto me, all ye that labour and are heavy laden, and I will give you rest. Take my yoke upon you, and learn of me; for I am meek and lowly in heart: and ye shall find rest unto your souls" (Matthew 11:28, 29).

What a way to get a crowd! People will stand in line for hours to have hands laid on them if you will assure them this will remove their inner turmoil and give them peace and rest. Few things in life are more restless than religion, and its only answer to this restless-ness seems to be activity. However, its solution becomes its greatest problem.

Jesus said the best way out of this restless activity was to become yoked to Him in an abiding relationship. This is a conundrum, for how can I rest yoked with a worker such as Jesus? Yokes are for working two animals together, not for resting.

In this parallel does Jesus mean rest? You may have noticed that the thrust of Scripture does not equate rest with inactivity but with directed activity. We rest not by ceasing to labor but by laboring effectively so that less human energy is expended and more divine power is utilized.

When we accept the invitation of Jesus to put our neck into the yoke with Him, we can be assured that our activity is going to be directed. We will begin to learn of Him—not about Him. Just as the younger animal learns by being yoked with the experienced ox, so we will learn how to minister under God's direction by being yoked to His favorite burden bearer, Christ Jesus.

Probably the first lesson we will learn is that the yoke is too big for us. It is His yoke. We'll have to stand on tiptoe just to hold our end up. We are no longer merely dealing with human needs whose yoke easily fits our standing, but we are dealing with God and His works of righteousness which will cause us to stand tall in faith at all times.

The second bit of wisdom we will acquire in a hurry is that when He begins to move, we had better move with Him, or we will get a plow right up our spine, because things move when God moves, and everything attached to Him begins to go forward. There will not be time to run it through a committee or even take a vote among the other oxen. When Jesus moves, move! The disciples were taught to pray, "Thy will be done in earth, as it is in heaven" (*see* Matthew 6:10). Heaven does not operate as a democracy; it is a theocracy. There are no boards, committees, councils, or vestries with whom God consults. He speaks, and it is done. Will the church on earth ever learn this sort of obedience? Yes, if they get yoked with Christ they will learn it if for no other purpose than to preserve themselves. When God says "Forward," Christ responds immediately and pulls along anything that is harnessed to Him.

A third instruction we learn is that when He stops, we might as well stop with Him, for all we will gain by pushing to go when He isn't moving is sore shoulder muscles. This is a hard lesson for the religious to learn. Somehow, we never allow God to stop doing something that He began in the past. We seem to feel that everything God does is purposed for perpetuity. How many of the programs of our churches are empty and lifeless but enthusiastically maintained because decades back in our heritage God used them in some special fashion? He may not have used this one in 300 years, but we are keeping it perennial because it is sacred and hallowed. We pour millions of dollars into it and expend the strength and energies of thousands of people in spite of the fact it has been totally unproductive since God stopped using it.

Some years ago, while I was pastoring a church in Eugene, Oregon, I sought the Lord for a program that would reach our young people more effectively than the denominational program we had been using for some years. God mercifully directed our hearts into a program that revitalized our youth and really turned them on for God. Many other pastors wanted to copy our program. After a year or so of this program, God spoke to me and said that He was through with it and for me to give it up. I couldn't bring myself to do so. God had shown it to me in prayer, had blessed it in its operation, and nothing had ever worked so well for us. For several weeks, God told me He was about through with it. When I saw the glory depart from it, I was happy to help bury it and to seek the face of the Lord for new direction and a fresh new program. When He stops, we stop.

A fourth message we cannot help but receive, when yoked together with Him, is to eat and drink when He eats and drinks, for we can never force His neck to lower when our appetite or thirst calls for quenching. How wonderful to learn that the ideal time to pray is when the Spirit within us wants to pray, and that when the Spirit wants to read the Word, that's the time to push other things aside to read. For on those occasions, the water will be still, cool, and pure, and the Word will glisten with tasty morsels of God's rich food. When He is drinking, the waters seem to be flowing from God. If I wait until I am released from the yoke, I will drink from stagnant cesspools. When He is feeding, it seems that every page of the Scriptures is alive, understandable, and full of truth applicable to my soul. When I refuse to eat with Him and choose my own feeding times, I exist on trodden straw or moldy grain.

It seems that all I have to do is set up a schedule for eating and drinking of Spiritual provisions, and I discover that my Yokefellow is not on the same schedule. As a matter of fact, He isn't even in the same time zone I am. If I determine that from nine to ten will be prayer time, more than likely He will awaken me at six saying, "I want to pray now." If I insist that I have scheduled prayer for nine, He leaves me alone to go back to sleep and has communion with the Father without me, for the Spirit does not need my help to pray; I need His help. But when my scheduled time for prayer rolls around, it is difficult, dry, unmeaningful, and unproductive, for He is not praying; He is already at work, dragging me and the yoke with Him. I am trying to feed while being forced to work. I may glean an occasional mouthful of grass, but I've missed the banquet table.

Still a fifth thing to be learned is that when He turns, we had better turn with Him or we will have a miserably sore neck. If God has chosen to turn west while we insist upon retaining the northward course, we will find ourselves resisting God with all the energies that are supposed to be harnessed to help God.

Some years ago, I had the pleasure of spending most of a week with some of God's outstanding men of this generation. Among the topics of discussion was an attempt to find where God was taking us. Some plotted the route of God through history. Others recounted the more recent ways of the Lord. During the varied discussions, one brother plotted the course on a blackboard, drew a line through the dots he had drawn, and showed that God had been moving in a straight course for years, and, therefore, we could

project into the future and pretty well know where God was leading. It sounded great until one of the brothers asked: "What if He
decides to make a left turn?" What if? Is God bound to the routes
of the past? Is our religious heritage His boundary line? Of course
not. God is sovereign and He alone knows where He is headed
through this wilderness. He didn't lead the children of Israel in a
straight line from Egypt ᴖ Canaan, and He has not promised a
straight line for us. At any point, He may very well do a ninety-
degree turn either to the right or to the left, and unless we are
sensitive and obedient, we will find ourselves resisting God's route.
But as long as we wear His yoke, we need not concern ourselves
with where we are headed. We're just moving with God.

When God was moving us out of the religious into a more vital
relationship with Himself, in the church in Oregon, it seemed that
so many things that had become our security were swept aside. We
were perpetually involved with the new and the untried. Several
leading members of the congregation demanded that I tell them
where we were headed. I stalled for time and went to prayer. "Tell
them," God told me, "that they're just going with God." Amaz-
ingly, that totally satisfied them. We didn't know the route, but we
didn't need to know it; we were just walking with the Lord on His
pathway.

A sixth lesson to be learned, when yoked with the Lord, is to let
Him choose the implement for the day. Oh, how much damage has
been done in the work of the Lord because we have refused to be
hitched to anything but our specialty. I have seen entire harvests
lost because the man called to minister considered himself to be an
outstanding plowman and refused to be hitched to a reaper. He
proved himself to be an able plowman, for he plowed under a full
year's labor and destroyed the entire crop.

I have also watched while highly trained evangelists earnestly
sought to reap a harvest on soil that had neither been plowed nor
planted. Their efforts were equally wasted, although they did very
little damage to the work of others. How important it is that we

allow the "Lord of the harvest" (*see* Luke 10:2) to choose the tool for the day, be it plow, disc harrow, weeder, fertilizing rig, or combine. He knows what is needed; He knows how it is operated, and all we need is a willingness to join Him in pulling it.

Still a seventh principle to be learned by being yoked with the Lord is that His pace varies, and He doesn't always walk. He rests. He does not go all out continuously. Sometimes He seems to walk very leisurely, as though He is enjoying the scenery. Other times you would almost think Egypt's chariots were in pursuit the way He hastens His work. Then there are times when He doesn't seem to be doing anything at all. When we are yoked to Him, we learn to be as comfortable in not doing as we were in doing most feverishly, as long as the partner isn't doing anything. He is the trained worker; we are the trainee. He is the instructor; we are the instructed. If He is at rest, how foolish for us to be other than at rest with Him.

When we are working *for* God, in response to a precept, we are constantly ill at ease about the amount of work done. It never seems to be sufficient or efficient. Even when we have fully satisfied one need, there are thousands of other needs crying to us. But when we are working *with* God, our response is to a partner, and the responsibility is fully His. If He works, we work with Him. If He rests, we enter into His rest with great enjoyment. We have entered into His vision and have seen what He sees. We've shared His food and drink and have labored with Him in the heat of the day. Now we dare share some rest time with Him. We dare "come apart and rest a while" (*see* Mark 6:31) to prevent coming apart permanently. Directed inactivity is as spiritual as directed activity, and all who will bear His yoke must learn this. Sometimes the most spiritual thing a person can do is sleep or enjoy recreation or just take time to be with the family. When this is done under divine direction, it will not cost heaven's Kingdom any service, and it will enable us to be more productive servants when it is time to get back into the harness again. "He maketh me to lie down in green pastures . . ." (Psalms 23:2). As surely as in the music score, the rest is to be observed equally with the notes; so times of activity are made more meaningful by times of directed inactivity.

But only God seems to understand this. Few pastors who are self-motivated have learned this. They drive themselves mercilessly as though they already possessed their glorified bodies and were immune to fatigue. They generally are great achievers and often build great kingdoms but at a tremendous cost to their own health, their families, and the staff that works for them. And may God graciously have mercy upon anyone who chooses to become their disciple. If the master has not learned to rest, the disciple will never be allowed periods of change of pace. This is another of the inherent dangers of yoking ourselves to a man instead of to Jesus.

Of the disciples in the early church it was said: "They took knowledge of them, that they had been with Jesus" (*see* Acts 4:13). If today's present emphasis is not reversed, the world will only be able to testify that they can see that the disciples had been with Judson or Jones or Smith or whoever the discipler may have been. Is that the image God wants the world to see in His church? Of course not. But unless we again instruct people to take *His* yoke upon them, they will never learn of Him nor reveal Him and His ways to the world.

As brethren we can be yoked together with one another in ministry without difficulty if we have all been trained in Christ's yoke. If we genuinely know His ways, His words, and His works, we'll experience no difficulty working with a strange partner who has had the same training no matter what religious affiliation he may have, for we have learned to abide even in the yoke.

Still another level of service is seen in 1 Corinthians 3:16: "Know ye not that ye are the temple of God, and that the Spirit of God dwelleth in you?" It is impossible to think of a temple without thinking about worship, for the purpose of a temple is ministry unto God, not unto people. Even the Old Testament tabernacle in the wilderness existed so God could be worshiped and so that He could abide among His people. Although we use the word *tabernacle* to include the entire structure from the outer court to the holy of holies, the Scriptures clearly define the tabernacle as the inner white curtain that formed the ceiling of the holy place. Where God resided and where the priests worshiped Him is the place God called His tabernacle. Everything within that curtained enclosure was an act of service unto God.

Whereas the first level of service was to minister *for* God as a response to a precept, and the second level was to minister *with* God in response to a partner, this third level is to minister *unto* God in response to a person. As we begin to see the person of God, we are able to minister unto Him rather than on His behalf. The first is ministry in the outer court; the second is the ministry level of the inner court, but this third level is the ministry of the holy of holies. For in the holy of holies absolutely everything was done unto God. In there everything was performed as an act of worship. Everything was done unto His glory out of love motivation. All that was rendered was at His bidding to meet His needs.

Too often we find comfort in dividing ourselves into artificial groups suggesting that one group seems especially called to work *for* God, another *with* Him, and a few select saints have the calling to minister *unto* God. But the truth is that God wants us to learn, first of all, to minister *unto* Him so that we can get yoked and minister *with* Him so that if He chooses to send us out occasionally to work on our own, we will be good workers *for* Him.

In stating that we are the temple of God, it suggests that we are the place where high worship, or ministry on its highest level, will take place. Couple this with the statement of Revelation 1:6, "And hath made us kings *and priests* unto God and his Father . . ." (italics added), and the affirmation of 1 Peter 2:9, "But ye are a chosen generation, a *royal priesthood* . . . that ye should shew forth the praises of him who hath called you out of darkness into his marvellous light" (italics added), and we cannot escape the truth that we are both the place of worship and the performer of it. We are the temple and the priest of that temple. Worship in our temple cannot be done by another; it must be done by us. God residing in us by His Spirit wants to be ministered unto by us in us.

The entire tribe of Levi was set aside to minister for God in the outer court and served in well-defined groups from sunup to sundown. But it was only the specified high priest who came into the holy of holies to minister unto God. Evangelism and meeting needs can be done effectively with combined groups of workers, but true ministry unto the Lord is a very individual and personal act. It is one man ministering worship and adoration to his God in the secret chambers of His inner temple. Of course, I believe in united public worship, but if it reaches any height of spiritual glory, it will be through many "ones" worshiping individually although they may be expressing it unitedly.

Worship is basically God's Spirit being blessed by man's spirit and the resultant interaction. It becomes a time of intimate fellowship, close communion, and emotional exchange. It is devotional in nature, divine in character, and delightful in its execution. It elevates man to the highest possible level while still in his body without lifting him into the level of dangerous pride. It is a bringing together of two worlds, a blending of man's little kingdom into God's limitless Kingdom, thereby enlarging man while enriching God. It is always the lesser blessing the greater by the consent of the blessed. It quickly aligns man as the servant while exalting God as supreme, but does so in such a pleasant and honorable fashion that man doesn't feel devastated or debased. Conversely, worship so brings man into such a sense of oneness with God that he feels an exaltation in God he could never have experienced outside of God. Worship always lifts the worshiper to the level of the worshiped! How practical and profitable it is, then, for us to learn to minister *unto* God as the highest working of righteousness. All of heaven's righteous beings worship God continuously and loudly. It is the normal expression of right relationship to God in the heavens. May God speed the day when it will be considered the conventional expression of righteousness here on the earth, for then we will "abide in thy tabernacle" and be able to "speaketh the truth in his heart"

Saul of Tarsus was a very religious man, sincerely trying to produce righteousness with zealous works which included killing any he could find of the new sect called "those of the way." More zeal and self-motivation could hardly be found in any man. Zealously responding to his understanding of the Old Testament Scriptures, he became a very active worker *for* God. But en route to Damascus, he supernaturally met the Lord in an amazing confrontation that changed his life. Quickly getting yoked to the Lord, he was an apt student and became an outstanding worker *with* God. But in working with the Lord, he was introduced to the Father, as will all who get yoked with Jesus. From that moment on, Paul could not be content to minister *for* God or even simply *with* God; he thoroughly enjoyed ministering *unto* God. Throughout his epistles, we hear him singing unto God, giving thanks to the Father, rejoicing in the midst of tribulations and persecutions, praising Him, praying in the Spirit, and magnifying God in every glorious way. Paul found the entrance to the holy of holies and enjoyed ministering unto God.

As a worker for God, he was feared and dreaded, but as one who, by abiding in Christ, ministered unto God, he was beloved and much sought after. When his orientation was to needs such as keeping Judaism pure, his life affected a small core group, but when he learned to minister unto God, his influence began to touch the entire world and still does.

Every man that history records as having done something outstanding in the church of Jesus Christ was a yoked worshiper. It was out of a life of devotion that his ministry became so effectual. It was having touched God that gave him so much of God with which to touch the lives of men.

In Ezekiel 44, which speaks of a priesthood set apart to minister in the great temple envisioned by this prophet and which many think is the New Testament church, three classes of people are totally prohibited from ministering at any level. No one with an unchanged status ("no stranger") or unchanged state ("uncircumcised in heart, nor uncircumcised in flesh") can ever minister in God's priesthood (*see* v. 9). First there must be a work of righteousness in the individual, then a response to that righteousness in works.

A group of Levites is confined to minister as "keepers of the charge of the house" (*see* v. 14) as a penalty for their idolatry. They are allowed to be guards, caretakers, servants, and attendants and to do the work of the outer court, but they are specifically barred from any ministry in the holy place or the holy of holies (*see* vv. 10–14).

We read of a family of these priests called the sons of Zadok who are specifically invited to minister directly unto God. There are eight distinct ministries offered to them as a privileged duty. "They shall (1) come near to me (2) to minister unto me, (3) and they shall stand before me (4) to offer unto me the fat and the blood, saith the Lord GOD: (5) They shall enter into my sanctuary, (6) and they shall come near to my table, (7) to minister unto me, (8) and they shall keep my charge" (vv. 15, 16, numbers added). This requires a change in position—"come near to me . . . stand before me . . . enter into my sanctuary," a change in service—"offer unto me the fat and the blood . . . they shall keep my charge," and a change in fellowship—"come near to my table, to minister unto Me." Even those being penalized for departing from the ways of the Lord can do the outer court ministries, but those whom God has chosen to make righteous are invited into heaven's sanctuary to minister their worship and service directly unto God.

Of course, these priests did not live there. After a time of ministering before the Lord, they came out to minister to the people but with a different ministry than they had known before. "And they shall teach my people the difference between the holy and profane, and cause them to discern between the unclean and the clean"

(v. 23). Only one who has seen the true justice of God can ever administer justice to his fellowman. Only the person who has enjoyed the sacred courts of God can rightfully tell the difference between the sacred and the secular. It is the one who regularly ministers unto a righteous God who can administer righteousness to needy men. It has well been said, "The man who bows the lowest in the presence of God stands the straightest in the presence of sin." Having been in the presence of purity and having fellowshiped with the God of holiness, there can be nothing but contempt for sin in any of its lurid forms.

The man who would abide in God's presence must learn to enter that presence and abide to minister unto God. He will learn more about ministry in the presence of God in a few minutes than he will learn in most of our seminaries in a few years. Holiness, righteousness, justice, and mercy are all attributes of God's very nature and cannot be learned in a classroom environment or from a textbook, for they must be caught not taught. They are learned by being in the presence of God where they are not only observed but absorbed, not only considered but conferred.

The man who would speak righteously and justly must have participated in righteousness and justness, for our lips only communicate what our lives have experienced. An adjusted walk that brings us into an abiding relationship with God will automatically change our manner of speaking.

4
Adjusted Words Aid Abiding

He that . . . speaketh the truth in his heart.

If, as the Scripture affirms, "Of the abundance of the heart his mouth speaketh" (*see* Luke 6:45), then conversation is a fluoroscope of the soul. To listen knowledgeably to a man talk is to learn a great deal about him, whether he wants to reveal himself or not. He may carefully choose his words to conceal his inner feelings or thoughts, but may very well give them away with his gestures, tone of voice, or the things he leaves unsaid.

James tells us that although man has tamed virtually every creature God made, he has not yet mastered his own tongue (*see* 3:8). Nor will he discover how until he learns to control his life, since the tongue is simply the communicative expression of the entire man.

It is worth noting that of all the varied ways the Holy Spirit could have demonstrated His presence in the life of the early church, He chose to do it through man's tongue. The Spirit took dominion over the very organ that man cannot control, speaking words the man was totally unable to utter. Far beyond the personal edification of this glossolalia (*see* 1 Corinthians 14:4) was the ecstasy of discovering that even the tongue could be mastered and used by God. For it is likely that what comes out of our lips becomes the greatest hindrance to remaining in the presence of God. More of us have talked our way out of God's presence than have ever walked out of His presence. Far too frequently I have seen a service that had risen into high spiritual realms unceremoniously dumped back into empty ritualism by the words of the leader. I have seen glorious praise sessions totally ruined by someone insisting on talking about fleshly things during the heights of spiritual glory. While our words of praise may lift us into God's presence, words of pride will quickly drop us back into carnality.

Little wonder, then, that Psalm 15 lists as the third area of needful adjustment: "He that . . . *speaketh* the truth in his heart."

Far too few of us realize the tremendous power—veritable creative power—that is vested in our speech. During His days on earth, Jesus cursed a fig tree for not bearing figs. The next day the disciples marveled that the tree had actually withered from the roots up. In answer to their amazement, Jesus said: ". . . Have faith in God. For verily I say unto you, That *whosoever shall say* unto this mountain, Be thou removed, and be thou cast into the sea; and shall not doubt in his heart, but shall believe that those things *which he saith* shall come to pass; he shall have *whatsoever he saith*" (Mark 11:22, 23, italics added). This, of course, presupposes a will that is submitted to God's expressed will but teaches that there is performing power available to the man who will speak in faith.

We've learned that faith comes when God speaks to us (*see* Romans 10:17), but do we sufficiently realize that faith is released when we say to the problem what God said to our spirit? It is not what we know that releases faith but what we say. It is not thinking about the need for the mountain to move but saying to the mountain, "Be thou removed and cast into the sea," that gets the job done.

The man who practices this will not only be powerful but peculiar, for he will find himself talking to unusual objects. Jesus did. Christ spoke to fish, wind, waves, dead men, a dead woman, a fig tree, and even to demons. The surprising part is that they all obeyed Him. Fish jumped into nets at His command on at least two different occasions. The fish with the gold coin swallowed Peter's hook. The wind and waves calmed instantly at Christ's voice. The dead came back to life when He called. Demons departed and trees withered when He spoke, for He spoke a word of faith—the creative word—He had heard His Father speak.

If God has spoken to our heart about a situation, we shouldn't simply repeat it to God, we should speak God's word to the situation and watch it obey His word. Man is the only portion of God's creation that rebels at the voice of God. Everything else—including the satanic—obeys God's commands.

When Moses appeared before Pharaoh, on numerous occasions, to declare the Word of the Lord, things happened. Although Pharaoh repeatedly refused to obey, he accepted the message as coming from God.

Plagues occurred at the word of Moses. It was the word to Pharaoh and the rod in the sight of the people, but miracles took place in rapid-fire order. Even through the services of an interpreter, the words of Moses were powerful and terrifying, very much as in years that followed the words of Elijah were to King Ahab when Elijah confronted that evil king with the words: "As the LORD God of Israel liveth, before whom I stand, there shall not be dew nor rain these years, *but according to my word*" (*see* 1 Kings 17:1, italics added).

These men spoke with authority, and what they said came to pass. The Bible is full of such examples. The men were generally called prophets—one who speaks for God—and were often feared greatly by the kings. They heard God speak within themselves and dared to declare it to others, and it came to pass!

There is tremendous power in our speech. Proverbs 18:4 says: "The words of a man's mouth are as deep waters. . . ." It is disappointing that most of us live on the shallow surface of these great depths of spiritual energy, stored up in the Holy Spirit who dwells within us, without ever exploring beneath that surface. God, who created the whole world with His voice, wants to speak creative, regenerative, life-giving words to and through us. He wants us to learn to speak what He is saying, not what we are thinking; what He is feeling, not what we are fearing.

On two or more occasions in my father's ministry, he rebuked the power of death and restored the individuals back to health. The one that made the greatest impression upon my boyish mind was when Dad responded to the pleading by a distraught wife who asked him to visit her dying husband in a hospital in a neighboring town. It was several hours before Dad arrived, and the doctor was just leaving the man's room. He told Dad that it was too late, but Dad pressed himself into the room anyway, followed by the doctor.

"Reverend," he said, "they don't get much deader than this. Look!" Flicking his cigarette lighter into a flame, he lifted the man's eyelid and held the flame close enough to burn the eyelashes. Putting away the lighter, he put one finger on the eyeball, and thumped it with a finger from the other hand.

"There's absolutely no life response, Reverend. He's gone."

But while the doctor was proving his point the Spirit was speaking within Dad saying, "Command him to awaken and live." Dad kept hoping the doctor would leave so he could obey the Lord, but the doctor was equally anxious to get Dad out of the room. The conflict within my father was strong, for he was a very gentle man and rarely lifted his voice against anyone or anything. But the Spirit was speaking so strongly within him that he ignored the doctor and firmly stated: "Wake up and live."

The doctor's snicker was lost in the voice of the man from the bed saying, "Why don't you two get out of the room and let me get some sleep!"

That man is still alive as of this writing—some forty years later.

Another occasion occurred when Dad was pastoring in Ukiah, California. During a Sunday service one of the elderly ladies, who had been very active in this young church, collapsed and died. The Spirit spoke within Dad and told him to rebuke the power of death.

Dad's first response was that she had lived her life and that this was probably her time to go. But the inner promptings of the Spirit were so strong that, contrary to Dad's nature, he literally leaped off the platform, across the altar area, and with his arm extended towards the collapsed form on the floor commanded, "Death, in the name of Jesus I rebuke you and deprive you of this victim." The lady began to stir, breathe normally, and gave this testimony to the church.

"I felt myself leave my body," she said, "and knew that I had died. I expected to ascend into heaven but felt myself descending toward hell. Only then did I realize that I was lost. I had been in religion for most of my life but had never accepted Jesus Christ as my Lord and Savior. The horror of being lost was sweeping through my whole spirit when I faintly heard the voice of Pastor Cornwall rebuking death. My downward course was stopped, and, when I looked back, I could see the saints gathered around my body, and I could see the pastor coming toward my body with that finger pointed right at me as he again rebuked death. Then I felt myself being squeezed back into my body and, well, here I am. God has given me another chance to get saved."

That lady remained alive, well, and active in that church as a true saint instead of a pretending saint, long after my father had moved to another pastorate.

But what if Dad had refused to say what God was saying within him? What if the doctor had intimidated Dad? What if fear of failure in front of his congregation had caused Dad to pray to God in the face of death instead of commanding death to release its prey as God had told him?

Dare we weaken the force of what God says to us or allow ourselves to be intimidated into complete silence? We can have what we say, not simply what we hear God say. There is a confession of faith that releases God's creative power on our behalf, and the man who yearns to abide in God's tabernacle must learn to speak what God is saying.

Obviously, if there is power for good in our words, there must also be power for evil in our speech. "Thou art snared with the words of thy mouth, thou art taken with the words of thy mouth" (Proverbs 6:2).

Words of anger create emotions of anger which often become actions of anger. Speaking lustfully creates sensuous desires, and often is the beginning of immorality, as witness the results of the widespread distribution of pornographic literature in the past few years.

Improper attitudes may poison the individual, but when they are put into speech, they often pollute and injure others. Many married persons have lived to regret hasty words of accusation spoken to their partners in a moment of anger. The bitterness of the feeling passes, but the wound created by the word lives on and on. How different the world would be if the thoughts of Lenin, Hitler, Mussolini, and more recently, Castro, had never been put into words to incite whole nations into military action.

How different the church would be if the words of modernists, liberals, agnostics, and religious empire builders had not been substituted for the Word of God in our pulpits and classrooms.

The declaration "Be not deceived: evil communications corrupt good manners" (1 Corinthians 15:33) is a powerful truth.

I recently appeared on a Christian television talk show as a cohost. One of the guests that day had been a brilliant criminal attorney for many years. His academic credentials and his list of professional achievements were outstanding. But he appeared on the show to testify how God had delivered him from a federal penitentiary after serving a brief portion of a ninety-nine-year term. He said that as a criminal lawyer he obviously associated with criminals, for they were his clients. They spent much time in his office discussing their activities. Slowly he found himself accommodating the things they were saying. Surprisingly enough, he began coaching them in their planning and showing them how to circumnavigate the law. The next step was to assist them in securing weapons for major jobs and, finally, in actually flying in narcotics from Colombia, South America.

When he was caught and convicted, he was about as incredulous as the sentencing judge that he, who was trained and sworn to uphold the law, had so flagrantly violated the law. On network television he said: "It all started when I began to listen to criminal talk. In hearing and talking those things they became common, and when they became common they seemed convenient, and when they became convenient they corrupted me to the point where I lost track of right and wrong."

It would do us well to be very careful what we listen to, what we watch, and what we say, for the power of words gets to us, as many of us have learned after buying something we really didn't need just because a salesman was clever in his use of words. David said: "Set a watch, O LORD, before my mouth; keep the door of my lips. Incline not my heart to any evil thing, to practise wicked works with men that work iniquity . . ." (Psalms 141: 3, 4). Some years back when I was honestly striving to step out of exaggerative speech, I repeatedly sang this passage, but I discovered that God's first action was not to put a padlock on my lips but blinders on my eyes and earplugs in my ears. He chose to deal with the input, not the output, of my speech, for what comes out of the mouth reflects what comes into the mind through other channels. As we guard what we watch and hear, we do not have much difficulty guarding what we say and do. Repeated viewings of violence, lust, and sin will automatically have a corrupting influence upon our thoughts, speech, and actions, while consistent time in God's Word and prayer and praise will have a cleansing and life-producing effect within us.

What we speak not only reflects what is in us but greatly reinforces it. Until it is spoken, it may well be nebulous, but once it is spoken, it tends to become definitive. That is why the Word calls for a confession of faith, not simply an acknowledgment of faith. "That if thou shalt confess with thy mouth the Lord Jesus . . . thou shalt be saved" (Romans 10:9).

Since all speech begins as a thought—first meditation then communication—it should be expected that at the outset Psalm 15 would deal with inner, nonverbal speech—that communicating we do with ourself. God wants the nature of our thought patterns about ourselves and the level of our self-appreciation to be truthful and honest. "He that speaketh the truth in his heart shall dwell in thy holy hill."  Too many of us confuse self-love with pride and erroneously feel that self-depreciation will produce humility. But God calls for a sane, balanced, and honest acceptance of ourselves, especially the self we are becoming in Christ Jesus. We must learn to love what He loves, including ourselves.

David said: "Behold, thou desirest truth in the inward parts: and in the hidden part thou shalt make me to know wisdom" (Psalms 51:6). Inner truth is God's desire for His people; yet few seem to achieve it. In our world of role playing, it seems easy to lose touch with our true inner self. How many thousands have never successfully answered the question "Who am I?" In the confusion of their never-ending search they often involve themselves in behavior keyed for self-destruction, whether it be excessive work, play, sex, or drugs.

To substitute a role in life for life itself is to live in utter confusion and, generally, to get lost in that role. There seems to be a nearly endless profusion of books about Marilyn Monroe, although her suicide is now many years old. She played her role well as America's sex goddess but couldn't seem to find herself as a real person. After these many years, it cannot simply be morbid curiosity that sparks the sale of so many books about her; there must be thousands of people who relate to her identity problem—people who have gotten lost in playing their roles as wife, mother, husband, father, provider, or protector. After a while, as with a stage actor in a lengthy run of a show, our role becomes perfunctory, and we have difficulty continuing to identifying with it.

This happens to Christians, too. If they never genuinely find themselves as a person in Christ, they weary of the role of being a Christian and seek personal identification in something else. Something within them rebels at merely being a doer of things; they yearn to be something or somebody. They scream for identification and long to know the truth about the "inner me."

What is the actual truth about the real us?

Jesus made two positive statements about truth. He stated: "I am the way, the *truth,* and the life" (*see* John 14:6, italics added), and He declared: "Thy word is truth" (*see* John 17:17). Jesus, the living Word, is the truth, and the Bible, the written Word, is the truth. The truth is not necessarily a right correlation of facts; the truth is a person, the Lord Jesus Christ Himself. The truth is the written or the living Word of God.

So in saying that God "desires truth in the inward parts," David is calling for meditation on Christ and His Word in the inward parts. And what a transformation it makes; what revelation it brings when we are musing upon Christ and thinking about His Word.

When we begin to listen to what God says about us instead of what people say about us or what we think of ourselves, we are on our way to true self-discovery. God, who made us, has written an instruction book about us that well describes us. It is called the Bible, but could very well have had the longer title *The Description of the Nature of Man and a Manual of Instructions for His Operation.*

Because sin has so darkened our minds and deceived our understanding, even the born-again child of God often is unaware of who he is, but God's Spirit and His Word abundantly reveal this to man. The Word declares us to be "sons of God" (*see* Romans 8:14), "heirs of God" and "joint-heirs with Christ" (*see* Romans 8:17), "children of God" (*see* Romans 8:16), "kings and priests unto our God" (*see* Revelation 1:6), and "elect of God, holy, and beloved" (*see* Colossians 3:12). This is a far cry from our singing, "I'm only a sinner, saved by grace." Don't you believe it! God never mentions our sin once it is confessed to Christ. He calls us sons, not sinners. He doesn't speak of us as objects of His grace as much as objects of His love. He doesn't speak as much of our condition as He speaks of our position in Christ.

How differently we see ourselves from the way God sees us. We see ourselves positioned in the world; God sees us positioned in "heavenly places in Christ Jesus" (*see* Ephesians 2:6). We think of ourselves as improving sinners; God thinks of us as immortal saints (*see* 1 Corinthians 1:2). We see ourselves as hopeless debtors to God, while He sees us as "heirs of the kingdom" (*see* James 2:5), and we think of ourselves as unprofitable servants, while He sees us as His unspotted bride (*see* Song of Solomon 4:7).

We do well to realize that God is not a flatterer and is totally incapable of lying. He does not say these things just to make us feel good; He is revealing our inner self to us. He is telling us what we are like, once the principle of sin has been eradicated from our nature.

Discovering what we are becoming in Christ enlarges our self-concept and strengthens our self-esteem. Knowing that God is not judging us for our present condition but from our future position causes us to believe that we are useful in His work and in His Kingdom.

The man who would learn to abide in the presence of God must learn to "speaketh the truth in his heart." He must say to himself what God has said about him. He must fill himself with Scripture, not self-depreciation. He must accept Divine instruction, not introspection. He must accept heaven's evaluation, not the human estimation. He will accept that "The heart is deceitful above all things, and desperately wicked: who can know it?" (Jeremiah 17:9) and trust the words of the Holy God who is "a discerner of the thoughts and intents of the heart" (*see* Hebrews 4:12).

It is simply a matter of accepting and believing what God says about us. If He calls an action or attitude a sin, we'll stop calling it an error, mistake, or a failing and join Him in saying that it is sin. If He says we are righteous, no matter how we may feel, we'll say what He is saying. We'll stop introspectively seeking something wrong within ourselves and wait until He points it out and simply confess it. Until then, we'll live in harmony with God's appraisal of our lives, for we are His beloved, living under His protection, enjoying the fullness of His provision, secure in His love, and declared to be His special people in this world and in the world to come. No amount of His training, correction, or chastisement will ever change what we are in Christ; it will only help us function more harmoniously with that position.

I am a P.K. (preacher's kid). I can well remember Mother's regular lecture to her five children before the family left for a church service. "Children," she would say, "I want you to remember that your father is the pastor of this church, and as such, is an example to the flock. His entire household is also an example. I expect you to behave yourselves as children of the pastor, and if your behavior is an embarrassment to his position, I will thoroughly spank you when we get home."

And believe me, it was no idle threat! She followed through often with Dad's able assistance. But even when I was being soundly whipped, I knew it did not threaten my position as preacher's son; it was simply dealing with my behavior as the preacher's son.

While our behavior does not change our position in Christ (short of apostasy and denial of the truth), our heavenly position should greatly affect our behavior.

Not only will meditating on God's Word and heeding the inner voice of the Spirit bring us to a sane acceptance of who we are in Christ, as opposed to the superspiritual pride of some or the subnormal self-abhorrence of others, but it will produce at least three valuable by-products in our lives.

The first of these is simply "The truth shall make you free" (*see* John 8:32). Embracing the truth inwardly brings liberty to the entire life. I believe in true deliverance ministries and rejoice in the testimony of one set free through such ministry. But I am convinced that Christians who are standing in lines to be set free through the laying on of the hands of another could be set free in the privacy of their homes if they would fill their minds with God's truth as much as they have filled themselves with books on demonology. We will not be set free by knowing our enemy; we will be set free by knowing our deliverer, the Lord Jesus Christ!

In a congregation I pastored some time back, I had a man with a besetting sin that became an upsetting situation in his home. After helping this brother out of this sin on two or more occasions, only to see him fall back into it again, I had a talk with his wife, asking which magazines he was reading, which television programs he watched, and which type of music he habitually listened to. When she listed the areas of his mental input, I told her I was going to loan them several cassettes filled with singing Scriptures. I asked that she substitute these for the music he usually listened to and asked that she insist that he play one of these cassettes in the car every time he drove. I further instructed her that every time she saw him reading one of his favorite magazines, she would gently interrupt by telling him how wonderfully God had made His Word come alive to her that day and then by reading that passage to him, preferably from one of the modern language translations.

She pointed out the penalties she would likely be subjected to if she so forcibly intervened in his personal life, but I countered by pointing out that unless he was permanently freed from this area of sin, the home was going to break up anyway.

I said that he had to start filling himself with the truth of God rather than his failures, fears, phobias, or lustful dreams.

It worked! As he filled his mind with the Word of God, it brought him complete and permanent freedom from that driving sin that had nearly destroyed his marriage.

"The truth shall make you free," not only from sin and Satan but from fear. The greatest fear in human experience is the fear of the unknown. God's truth reduces the field of the unknown by revealing the things of God, the things of the demonic, and the things of man. We can always depend upon the unfailing accuracy of God's truth. No matter what demons may say, or what input our sensory nature may make to our intellect, God's Word will always be correct. By filling our heart with God's truth, we immunize ourselves against the fear of the supernatural, the abnormal, the unusual, or that which seems to be extrasensory, for facts are always the best answer to fancy and fear.

The truth also sets us free from falsehoods and half-truths, which are the most dangerous form of lies. No lie can successfully contend with revealed truth. The scriptural answer to Satan's temptation has always been: "It is written" (*see* Matthew 4:4). It is not that quoting the Scriptures is going to scare Satan, for he rebelled at the living Word, why should he bow to the written Word? But when the devil speaks or entices us, our best defense is to embrace the truth of God's Word. We'll not be deceived if we know God's truth and receive it.

Oh, the religious darkness that has been broken by the penetrating light of God's divine truth. Who can count the shackles that have been loosed when God's Word screamed, "Let my people go, that they may serve me" (*see* Exodus 8:1)? Superstition, spiritual servility, ceremonial substitutions, and sectarianism release their prisoners when the truth is embraced.

True freedom of worship is a by-product of "speaking the truth in your heart."

A second by-product of "speaking the truth in your heart" is an inner work of sanctification. In Jesus' high-priest prayer to the Father He says: "Sanctify them through thy truth" (*see* John 17:17). Although volumes have been written on this theme, and entire denominations have been built around it, the simplest possible definition of sanctification merely is "set apart from and set apart unto." All the vessels and implements used in worship in the Old Testament tabernacle were said to be sanctified. That is, they were set apart from secular use and set apart unto divine use.

The church I am associated with in Tabb, Virginia, has a plurality of elders. At the present there are four of us doing the work of the ministry. Each was flowing in ministry in this local area before being set apart as elders in the church. A few wives in the congregation have expressed their opinion that an injustice has been done in not appointing their husbands to the eldership. I have assured them that it would be my personal delight to wash the feet of their husbands and ordain them as elders just as soon as I see the ministry of an elder flowing through them. And being received by the congregation for ordination does not set a person aside unto the ministry, it only recognizes what God has done. God chooses His own workmen. "The LORD hath set apart him that is godly for himself" (*see* Psalms 4:3). God has never operated with volunteer workers; He conscripts His workmen from the ranks of the available.

I have suggested to each of these ambitious wives that if she genuinely feels that her husband should be an elder, she should encourage and assist her mate to fill himself with the Word of God, for God sanctifies with His truth. Get him to think the Word, speak the Word, pray the Word, communicate the Word, live the Word, and sing the Word until God's truth is in his conscious mind, his subconscious mind, his dreams, his ambitions, and his conversations, and God will very likely set him apart unto Himself. Then the people will recognize it, and the eldership will respond to it with ordination.

The same principle applies to all who would aspire to public ministry at any level. Fill yourself with God's Word. Don't worry so much about the techniques of preaching; concern yourself with having something to say. Don't try to gain man's ordination by going to his school and joining his Christian organization; seek God's sanctification, His setting apart, unto the ministry. The last thing the church needs today is more novices practicing on her. What is needed is more teachers of the Word—more men and women who have filled their lives with the Sacred Writ and can say with assurance, "Thus saith the Lord."

Businessmen need not quit their businesses to enter the ministry. If they fill their lives with the ministry of the Word, then share it wherever they go—gently and progressively—this living Word will set them apart unto God's service. Their ministry will make room for them, and they will find themselves being phased out of the business world and into the ministerial field. God's Word—read, received, believed, and expressed—will do its own sanctifying.

The third by-product of "speaking the truth in your heart" is that it strengthens the inner man. Paul the Apostle speaks of our being "nourished up in the words of faith and of good doctrine" (*see* 1 Timothy 4:6). We desperately need to be nourished and strengthened by words of faith and words about God. We not only need to get into the Word, but to get the Word into us.

We rarely open a hymnbook in our church, and only occasionally do we sing a gospel chorus. We prefer to sing the Scriptures. As valuable as the poetic expression of the experiences of others may be, nothing compares with God's Word for encouragement, comfort, instruction, and edification. Singing about heaven, home, and mother may draw a crowd for a quartet concert, but it does very little to build up, strengthen, or nourish man's spirit, but singing God's Word will accomplish all this for His Words are life-giving (*see* Psalms 119:50).

Whether we sing the Word, say it, quote it, read it, memorize it, or listen to it being preached, we will be made strong by it as surely as a healthy body is nourished by wholesome food.

But learning to speak correctly to and about ourself ("speaking the truth in his heart") is only the beginning for the one who aspires to "dwell in thy holy hill." The second area of speech that needs adjustment, in order to abide in God's presence, is the way we speak *about our neighbor.* "He that backbiteth not with his tongue . . . against his neighbour" (*see* Psalms 15:3).

The Hebrew word used here for backbiting is *ragal* which means "slanderer or talebearer" and is the way the Living Bible translates it: "Anyone who refuses to slander others, does not listen to gossip, never harms his neighbor."

Solomon warns us: "The words of a talebearer are as wounds, and they go down into the innermost parts of the belly" (Proverbs 26:22).

The basic problem with slander and talebearing is that they do not require facts, only a willing listener. How frequently has the reputation of a saint of God been tarnished, and even tarred, by someone expressing his thoughts and suspicions to a friend, who added her thoughts to it before passing it on, until by the time it got back to the original speaker it was impossible to recognize and equally impossible to refute? This preoccupation with gossip and slander is often an indication that the gossipers have chosen not to acknowledge God in their lives anymore. Romans 1:28–30 is translated in the Berkeley Bible: "Just as they did not see fit to acknowledge God anymore, so God gave them over to depraved thoughts, to practice what is not decent, because they have been filled with every sort of wickedness, immorality, depravity and greed; crammed with envy, murder, quarreling, deceit, and malignity; as gossips, slanderers, God-haters; insolent, proud, and boastful; inventors of evil; disobedient to parents; without conscience, fidelity, natural affection or pity."

We get some insight into God's view of gossip and slander by seeing where He classifies the gossipers and slanderers. Little wonder, then, that it will disqualify us from an abiding relationship with God.

About three years ago I began to receive cancellations of conferences and convention speaking appointments. The reasons given sounded like weak excuses, but I didn't pursue the issue. Finally a pastor, with whom I had ministered repeatedly, phoned me to say he was shocked that in the many times I had been in his church I had never mentioned being a divorced person. I assured him I had not mentioned it because it was not true, but he insisted that he had heard it from a very reliable source. I offered to put my wife on the phone or to send him a photostatic copy of our marriage license before he would accept the truth. So widely has it been circulated that Reverend J. Cornwall is a divorced man that I've had to rewrite my biographical sketch to assure ministers that I am indeed the husband of one wife.

Unusual? Not at all. The more a person is in the public eye, the more widespread will be the slander and talebearing about him. Berekely translates Numbers 14:36: ". . . starting a whispering campaign. . . ."

It's tragic when saints get involved in idle rumors and slanderous stories; yet it is more common than it should be, for it is a major cause of losing our standing in the presence of God.

It is not too unusual for Christians, when leaving glorious church services where the presence of God was manifestly present, to congregate at a convenient restaurant for fellowship and food. Often the conversation shifts from the sweetness of the service to small talk about the mundane. Inevitably someone injects a juicy bit of slander into the conversation, and the game of gossip flows through the restaurant. All sense of God's presence is lost; so much so that when they get home and choose to read from the Bible, before going to bed, they're amazed that there is no more glory, no sense of God's presence. The Word becomes like shredded wheat without milk or sugar, and their prayer seems to drop to the floor. How was it possible to have so fully enjoyed God's presence and then within the hour to be almost totally without spiritual contact? Slander did it! If we're going to talk like that about our brethren, we should expect to lose the flow of God's presence, for slander and gossip are contrary to God's nature. Heaven has none of it, and neither should the church.

The New Testament gives us two titles for our archenemy Lucifer. He is called Satan and devil. (*see* Revelation 12:9). The term *devil* comes from the Greek word *diabolos* which means "slanderer." He doesn't need the facts; he'll just slander on suspicion. Some Greek scholars translate the word "false accuser." He is expert at false accusation. He falsely accuses God to you, you to your brethren, your brethren to you, and you to yourself. He doesn't need, and should never have, the help of the saints to get his work of slander accomplished. Saints don't need to yak-yak about one another and share their have-you-heard suspicions. Even if the source who told the slander is known for his veracity, if we repeat it, we may become known for our audacity when it is found to be untrue. "He that uttereth a slander, is a fool" (*see* Proverbs 10:18).

Perhaps we need to review the three elementary rules that our parents taught us about conversation. First, is it true? Second, is it kind? And third, is it necessary? Even if we can back up the story with facts, is it necessary to tell it? Do we really need to display dirty linen in public?

Have you noticed that the moment God begins to discipline one of His children, the chastened one becomes the subject of gossip, slander, and talebearing? Psalms 69:26 is translated in the Amplified Bible: "For they pursue *and* persecute him whom You have smitten, and they gossip about those whom You have wounded, [adding] to their grief *and* pain."

When I lived at home, as a boy, it was absolutely forbidden to add to, extend, or even delight in any punishment meted out by my parents to any of us children. They said they would administer sufficient corrections and needed no help from us. Even passing on the information about a spanking to a family member who had been absent was to risk being spanked for talebearing.

Is it possible that God would administer more chastisement upon His sinning sons if He could trust the rest of His family to stay out of the disciplinary action?

Because of this matter of talking *about* our neighbor, the next statement made in Psalm 15 is: "Nor taketh up a reproach against his neighbor" (*see* v. 3). First, no backbiting; next, no reproach. The Hebrew word for reproach is *cherpah* which means "to expose or defame." In contrast to the slanderer, who needs no facts, the exposer or defamer must have the facts.

We saw that *devil* means slanderer, but Satan, which comes from the Greek word *Satanas,* means "adversary, or true accuser." He acts like a district attorney. If Satan can get the facts on a saint, he will do his utmost to destroy him and his standing before God. Satan doesn't need our help at all, but the accused saint does. "Let him know, that he which converteth the sinner from the error of his way, shall save a soul from death, and shall hide a multitude of sins" (James 5:20).

What is needed in the Body of Christ is conversion from sin, not conversation about sin. Much needless and often times irreparable damage has been done by forcing public confession of private sins. Confession and, where possible, restitution should be offered to the person or persons against whom we have sinned. But in making open and public confession of these private sins, we often project great condemnation and fear into the lives of the weaker saints and so damage our reputation that our ministry is destroyed among those same people. While God forgives and forgets, people don't.

I doubt if making a public example of a sinning brother will be as great a deterrent to sinning as it will be an impediment to confessing sin. It is the goodness of God that dissuades men from sinning, not fear of exposure by man. "The goodness of God leadeth thee to repentance" (*see* Romans 2:4).

Of course, I believe in church discipline. We probably have too little of it in these times. But when the Scriptures speak of bringing a matter before the church, I seriously doubt that it refers to bringing it before all who assemble in a public worship service. Don't we have some responsible brothers and sisters, call them any title you are comfortable with, who can handle these matters in love, compassion, and in privacy? Cannot the sinning saint find release through confession and guidance through counsel without the total loss of his standing among other saints? God has not called us either to slander or expose His children, but to cover and to love them back to a warm relationship with Himself. Solomon summarized it in saying: "A talebearer revealeth secrets: but he that is of a faithful spirit concealeth the matter" (Proverbs 11:13).

Interestingly enough, Berkeley translates Psalms 15:3: "who does not *carry scandal* concerning his neighbor," while the Living Bible translates it: "does not *listen* to gossip" (italics added). Apparently the Hebrew is translatable either way. The thrust of the truth seems to be that whether we carry the scandal or listen to it, gossip will keep us from abiding in God's presence. The listener is equally guilty with the speaker. If no one would listen, gossip and slander would disappear overnight. But I don't anticipate this happening this year, for too many who are afraid to participate in wrongdoing act out their fantasies vicariously in listening to the detailed stories of those who actually have sinned. Jesus taught that the desire to do was equal in guilt to having done it (*see* Matthew 5:28; 15:19).

Can we imagine, in our wildest flight of fancy, the angels, who stand in God's presence, whispering about the sins of the saints on earth? Of course not! Their goal is not to expose, but to expunge men's confessed sins with the blood of heaven's Lamb. Their commission is to get us through sin, not to damn us in the midst of it. They have greater things to talk about and listen to than our human weaknesses and failings. They've heard the song of Moses and the song of the Lamb (*see* Revelation 15:3) and cannot lower themselves to listen to sordid stories of sinning saints. They rejoice in our victory over sin (*see* Luke 15:10), and they weep at sin's victory over us. Should not the saints who are recipients of divine grace emulate the angels from whom grace seems to have been withheld?

Whether we are the teller or the "tellee"—the speaker or the listener—Jesus warned: "But whoso shall offend [literal Greek, 'to scandalize'] one of these little ones which believe in me, it were better for him that a millstone were hanged about his neck, and that he were drowned in the depth of the sea" (Matthew 18:6). It is better, in God's sight, that we die the slow death of drowning than we disgrace or scandalize one of God's children. He adds that offenses must come but "Woe to that man by whom the offence cometh!" (*see* v. 7).

If we want to learn to abide in the presence of God, we will have to discipline ourselves to leave righteousness and justice to God, to allow Him to chasten His children without our interference, and to stop trying to appear righteous by exposing the unrighteousness of others. We must learn to neither speak or listen to slander, gossip, backbiting, or talebearing as a matter of self-preservation, for the price of participation in them is the loss of the divine presence in our lives.

But this discipline will not only be self-protecting, it will also be self-perfecting for James observes: "If any man offend not in word, the same is a perfect man, and able also to bridle the whole body" (*see* James 3:2). The control of our lips and our life is interrelated.

According to Psalm 15 a third area of our speech that needs to be adjusted by God's Spirit, if we would learn the continual communion of God's presence, concerns our speaking *to the saints.* "He honoureth them that fear the LORD" (*see* v. 4). The Living Bible translates it, "Anyone who commends the faithful followers of the Lord." I prefer this translation because "to honor" may only be an attitude but "to commend" requires an expression of that attitude. No matter how highly we may feel about others, they are neither blessed nor aided until our attitude has been expressed.

We cannot measure the hours and days of depression, introspection, frustration, and futility that could have been spared if someone had expressed his commendation and appreciation to the saints.

All who serve in God's ministry are subjected to criticism, cynicism, and complaint on a rather regular basis. It is difficult to continue to believe in yourself when it seems that everything you do or say is wrong. An occasional word of approval or appreciation can go a long way to balance the disapproval of others. No one is perfect in his living and ministry; conversely, no one is entirely imperfect. All have something worth commending.

While writing this chapter, I spent some time in the home of a very godly saint who had invited her teenage nephew to spend a part of his summer in her home, hoping that the anointing of God that rested in the home would affect his life.

The home was very busy with preparations for a camp meeting, and repeatedly this boy was in the wrong place or doing the wrong thing, and it seemed that everyone in the home corrected him.

The second night of the camp meeting, this sister had several pastors come to her cottage for a snack and a time of fellowship. She was sharing with us some of the deep dealings of God in her life when the door opened and the nephew walked in. As she glanced at her watch, she looked at the boy and in the gentlest of tones said, "Thank you, Robert, for obeying me and coming in on time," and then continued her story to her assembled guests. I looked at Robert and saw a glow of satisfaction as he pulled up a chair to listen with the rest of us. The short expression of commendation made him feel welcomed and wanted. He belonged!

While God does chasten and correct us, for our own good, He also commends us for our development. He does not specialize in pointing out our weaknesses; He delights in pointing out our strengths. Even in the midst of our stumblings and strivings, He finds something worthy of commendation and encourages us on with praise.

This is also our responsibility. The New Testament calls for us to edify, exhort, and to "comfort one another with these words" (*see* 1 Thessalonians 4:18; 1 Corinthians 14:4). We need to learn sensitivity towards each other and to share a word of appreciation, commendation, and instruction.

Frequently in our congregation, we observe the Lord's Supper as a breaking-of-bread service. Each person is given a generous portion of a large loaf and encouraged to break bread with another, expressing love and appreciation. If forgiveness is needed, we are encouraged to ask for it, but our main intent is to release love and commendation to one another. We are encouraged to express appreciation to our parking-lot attendants, to the pianist and organist, to the ushers, and to the brothers in charge of the tape room. These serve without pay and often sacrifice part of the service to enable others to enjoy it fully. We're asked to consider a word of comfort for the widow, no matter how long she has lived alone, and love for the disabled and sickly. The aged in our midst need to know they are appreciated, and the youth need to know they are accepted.

We may feel all the right attitudes, but until they are expressed, they only benefit us. Expressed, they bring courage, comfort, and consolation to others.

As a pastor, I've watched the change in the demeanor of the divorcee, the unmarried, or the woman separated from her husband because of the service or his job, after a few of the men of the congregation spoke kindly to them. Not flirtatiously, but felicitously. They just needed a word of approval or appreciation from a man. The reverse is equally true. Men need commendation from women. It's a shame that Christians so fear lust that they cannot share family love. Proverbs says, "A word fitly spoken is like apples of gold in pictures of silver" (25:11) and "The words of the pure are pleasant words" (*see* 15:26).

We have further taught our congregation to save their small talk for unbelievers. When we gather together, we don't need to talk about golf scores, grandchildren, weather, or cars; we should learn to talk words of love, comfort, edification, and blessing. We need to share something from God's Word with each other since nowhere else in our life experiences are we getting words that build us up.

The minor prophet Malachi wrote: "Then they that feared the LORD spake often one to another: and the LORD hearkened, and heard it, and a book of remembrance was written before him for them that feared the LORD, and that thought upon his name. And they shall be mine, saith the LORD of hosts, in that day when I make up my jewels; and I will spare them, as a man spareth his own son that serveth him. Then shall ye return, and discern between the righteous and the wicked, between him that serveth God and him that serveth him not" (3:16–18).

God not only has the "book of life" (*see* Revelation 3:5), but has a "book of remembrance" in which is listed the names of every person who chose to talk about Him to other believers. How rare this form of conversation must be for God to list it in His diary!

He speaks of this list as an inventory of His jewels and says that in time of danger, they are the first of His possessions to be carried to safety. Rather than trying to escape coming judgments by fleeing to another locality, we would do well to develop the practice of talking the things of God to one another. That way we will be spared by God and need not try to save ourselves, for God has a book of those He intends to spare. He calls them jewels, as precious to Him as a serving son.

In this day of great religious deception and counterfeit, it is often difficult to tell the difference between the wicked and the righteous—the true servant of God and the false—but their speech will give them away. "Then shall ye return, and discern between the righteous and the wicked, between him that serveth God and him that serveth him not" by listening to them talk away from the pulpit. The unrighteous talk only of the mundane and the profane. We will discern by listening: "For by thy words thou shalt be justified, and by thy words thou shalt be condemned" (Matthew 12:37).

"Who shall abide in thy tabernacle? Who shall dwell in thy holy hill?" He who has made an adjustment in his speech so as to speak the truth in his heart, to speak no slander or defamation about his neighbor, and to speak words to honor, commend, and edify the saint.

Little wonder, then, that David prayed, "Let the words of my mouth, and the meditation of my heart, be acceptable in thy sight, O LORD, my strength, and my redeemer" (Psalms 19:14).

Our attitudes—inner meditations—will greatly determine the length of our sojourn in God's presence, for throughout the whole Bible, God deals more severely with attitudes than He does with actions. Religious actions that are not expressive of similar attitudes are totally rejected by God. Both our expressed words and our inner meditations must harmonize for us to be acceptable in God's tabernacle on an abiding basis.

5

An Adjusted Will
Aids Abiding

He that sweareth to his
own hurt, and changeth not.

Not only do the inner meditations—the unspoken thoughts—
affect the speech pattern, but they generally control the will. David
spoke his will into submission in declaring, "Bless the LORD, O my
soul: and all that is within me, bless his holy name" (Psalms 103:1).

God cannot let us abide continuously in an experience of
Emmanuel—God with us—until the controlling force of our life,
the will, has been brought into submission to the will of God, as
surely as our words were taught to conform to the Word of God.
But man's will can be harnessed to God's desires. This is the fourth
adjustment Psalm 15 requires as a prerequisite to abiding continuously in God's presence. "He that sweareth to his own hurt, and
changeth not" (*see* v. 4). The Living Bible translates it: "Keeps a
promise even if it ruins him." The man who sets his will to do the
will of God and doesn't change it even when it begins to cost him
something is on his way to abiding in God's holy hill.

Jesus told His disciples: "If ye know these things, happy are ye
if ye do them" (John 13:17). Happiness, contentment, or blessedness
does not come with increased knowledge but with an activated will.
It is what we do with what we know that sets the course of our life.

I once met a man with a Ph.D. degree who claimed to be proficient in seven languages; yet he earned his living installing and maintaining residential fences. Somehow he had never been able to make his vast knowledge work for him.

I have also met many Christians who were highly trained in the Scriptures and filled with spiritual principles but were also unable to make their vast knowledge work for them. In spite of all the books they had read and all the tapes they had listened to, they lived weak, anemic Christian lives.

If knowledge alone could produce spiritual relationship, then our seminary graduates would automatically be saints instead of merely educated men. But the tree of knowledge that was substituted for the tree of divine life in the Garden of Eden continues to be substituted in our churches and our religious schools. We still feel that knowing is an end in itself rather than a means to an end.

To further emphasize this principle, Jesus told the story about a farmer during the rush of harvest season who asked his two sons to help gather in the crop (*see* Matthew 21:28–31). One said an immediate yes, but never showed up in the field. The other son felt the request was belittling to his station as a son and refused to go. Later, however, he realized the urgency of reaping the harvest while it was ripe and unceremoniously joined the workmen in the field. Jesus then asked His disciples which of the two sons actually *did* the will of his father. Each son knew his father's will, but only the second son fulfilled it by bending his own will to submit to the will of the father. It is vitally important for us to learn to make our life conform to our lips and to adjust our will to the known will of God, for it is not sufficient to have learned to "speak the truth in our heart." We must also learn to follow through with that truth in our daily living.

This level of committed honesty is becoming very rare in our society, whether directed to our fellowman, ourself, or our God.

The expression "A man's word is his bond" is antiquated today. Even a man's signature is questionable security. It is amazing how many pages a group of lawyers will draw up in their attempt to write an ironclad contract and equally astounding how another group of lawyers will be able to find loopholes that allow the signer to be released from the contract. Even marriage vows are taken extremely lightly and broken almost at whim. Divorce has become commonplace with minimal penalty attached.

But one who would learn to abide in Christ, according to this passage, must learn honesty in all of his commitments. The American practice of telling people what we think they want to hear must be set aside for the scriptural principle of "Let your communication be, Yea, yea; Nay, nay" (*see* Matthew 5:37; James 5:12). If we don't mean it, we shouldn't say it. If we don't intend to do it, we shouldn't promise to get involved. Even when "my mouth overloads my back," I must follow through. I must make myself believable to myself, my fellowman, and to God.

It is imperative for us to learn to stand by commitments made unto ourself, otherwise commitments made to others will vacillate. Pledges for self-improvement need to be carried through. Vows to spend time in the Word and in prayer should not be subject to the caprice of the moment. One reason that correspondence schools are such a profitable enterprise in America is the very small percentage of students who complete the courses. The schools collect for the entire course of instruction, but need only a small staff to handle the workload, knowing that after the first month or two, most students drop out of the program.

Paul asked the church at Galatia, "Ye did run well; who did hinder you that ye should not obey the truth?" (Galatians 5:7). The number of people who confess Christ always greatly outnumbers those who live the Christian life. Many claim to have made a commitment of their life to Christ while, in fact, they merely took Christ on a trial basis. Their emotions may have opened, but their will didn't respond.

One of the contributing factors to this withdrawn commitment may be the embraced attitude that they must reject life from the moment they accept God. I had this problem. I was raised in a rather strong Victorian atmosphere with legalistic religious overtones that seemed to teach that anything I enjoyed was wrong. The motto of my life became: "Everything I like is either illegal, immoral, or fattening." This is not right, for God did not make us to be ascetics. The purpose of redemption is to enable us to live life to the fullest. Jesus said: "I am come that they might have life, and that they might have it more abundantly" (*see* John 10:10).

Yet many Christians are unduly introspective, continually condemning themselves, convinced that it would be wrong to enjoy anything in life, and feeling guilty about everything decent they may possess. How we need to achieve a balance between self-negation and self-exaltation. We do have a right and a responsibility to be a person, for only as a person can we worship or work for God. We dare not lose our identity in our search for spirituality.

I dare to believe that God enjoys life. I believe that amid the heartbreak of His short time on this earth, Jesus enjoyed parts of life to the fullest. Otherwise, why did He tell His disciples: "These things have I spoken unto you, that my joy might remain in you, and that your joy might be full" (John 15:11)? Masculine men forsook their trades to follow Jesus; yet women were comfortable in His presence, and even children enjoyed being around Him. This does not sound like a withdrawn, sad-faced ascetic who saw nothing but gloom and sin in this life. I think Jesus enjoyed being alive and wants us to enjoy life as well. We owe this commitment to ourselves.

How much more attractive the claims of Christ would be if more of His followers would learn to discipline themselves from sin without losing the zest for life. We need not cease living because of Christ's loving. His love should make life all the more beautiful for us.

Therefore, we should stop feeling guilty about having time for devotion, rest, family, friends, love, and recreation. We should not allow these times to be consistently intruded upon. "To every thing there is a season, and a time to every purpose under the heaven" (Ecclesiastes 3:1) declared Solomon.

Occasionally we need to be reminded that a commitment to Christ does not violate prior commitments, such as marriage and family responsibilities. Frequently, I find people who feel that their newfound relationship with Christ totally supersedes their marriage relationship, and they withhold themself from their mate or let the house and family go uncared for while they get deeply involved in the work of the church. Their excuse is that the work of the Lord comes first. While we do give Him first place, we do not give Him total place. Serving God cannot, and will not, be a substitute for fulfilling our roles in the home or in life.

Recently, I was pressed by letter and phone call to go to a southeastern conference grounds for a time of ministry with special emphasis placed upon counseling the key members of the staff. Because I could not go to them, I encouraged them to come to me, and one couple took time to spend a Sunday with me. They thoroughly enjoyed the morning service and then came to my home for the afternoon. They seemed to have deep spiritual problems. After listening to them for quite some time, I interrupted the wife to ask her how long it had been since she had done any baking. She looked shocked that I would ask such a nonspiritual question and let me know, in a gentle manner, that she gave herself to the study of the Word and to prayer.

I restated my question, but this time I addressed it to the husband.

"It has been many months," he said.

Then I asked him how long it had been since he had gone fishing, since he had remarked earlier how much he enjoyed that sport.

"Far longer than it has been since she spent time baking in the kitchen," he answered, "for we feel that the work of the Lord is too important for me to take time for fishing."

A few more such questions convinced me that the major part of the interpersonal problems the group was experiencing was neither demonic or spiritual. They simply had lost identity with life and in their commendable self-sacrifice had ceased to be real people. They had tried to be something else but did not know what it was they were trying to become.

I assured them that as surely as there must be time for the Word and prayer, time to teach and work, there must also be time to love, time to cook, time to fish, and time to just be people.

When the truth of this finally penetrated their defenses, the joy of the Lord filled both of them, and they declared: "We feel you have rescued us. Hallelujah!"

Rescued them? No, I had just reminded them that serving God did not invalidate all previous commitments.

In order to develop strength of character, a good parent insists upon his children fulfilling their promises. Would our Heavenly Father do any less in training His children? If God sees my inconsistency in keeping my word to myself or to those around me, will He not have grave reservations about any pledges I may make to Him? Honesty is developed in small areas of life, not in life's major issues.

Wisely, Solomon reminds us, "When thou vowest a vow unto God, defer not to pay it; for he hath no pleasure in fools; pay that which thou has vowed. Better is it that thou shouldest not vow, than that thou shouldest vow and not pay" (Ecclesiastes 5:4, 5). When we are dealing with Almighty God, who is truth (*see* John 14:6) and cannot lie (*see* Titus 1:2), we will be confronted with scrupulous honesty on His part that demands transparent honesty on our part.

How careful, then, we should be in making any form of a vow to God whether in a pledge, a prayer, or in singing a song, for we will be held accountable for it.

Madame Guyon wrote: "God extracts from us in time of peace that which we pledged Him in time of war." How quick I am to vow to God in the face of danger or need, and how easily I withdraw my pledge later with the weak excuse "I didn't see into the future to know it would be so difficult." But in God's sight a commitment is a commitment, and I am thankful that it is so. What if, in the midst of a time when I yield to the unspiritual life, God should say to me, "Judson, I'm going to have to withdraw my pledge to save you. I didn't realize how much work it would entail"? My entire security is dependent upon God's faithfulness to keep His Word.

Several years ago Brother Edward Miller got my attention by saying, "There are three things God is building into His church: faith, love, and inner honesty. Any one of the three will get a man through to heaven, but all three of them are necessary to become a man of God." Of the three, I've observed that inner honesty is the slowest to develop and the hardest to maintain; yet without it, I will be greatly limited in how high I can rise in God's presence or how long I can linger in His holy place.

But knowing all of this, why are we so slow to do what God has spoken? Jesus asked the question: "And why call ye me, Lord, Lord, and do not the things which I say?" (Luke 6:46). I've been in many conferences where every prophetic utterance was followed by a round of applause and little else. No one seemed concerned that the Lord may have called us to our knees for a time of repentance, or to our feet for a season of rejoicing. No matter what He said, they applauded and then continued to do their own thing.

God doesn't speak just to get three *whoopees* and two *happy-lujahs* out of us. He expects an obedient response.

How would we feel if when we instructed our child to close the front door, our command was met with, "Oh, goody! Daddy spoke to me! He has a wonderful voice, and if he didn't love me so much, he wouldn't bother to speak to me"?

We'd probably say, "Knock it off, Daughter, and shut the door." We were not seeking emotional response but obedient action.

So is God. Once He declares His will, it should almost automatically become our will. But such is seldom the case.

A classic example of this occurred when I was pastoring the

church in Eugene, Oregon. One Sunday evening, a guest arrived late for the service but entered into the worship very quickly. After the service he began to tell me the following story, which so amazed and delighted me that I called the people back to the auditorium and gave him the microphone so all could hear it.

He said, "I am Mr. Brown [not his true name], and I live in Portland, Oregon. For some time, my firm has been pressing me to move to the Eugene area to open a branch office for them, but I have staunchly resisted them because I own my own home in Portland, love my church, and have no desire to relocate.

"But about a week ago," he continued, "I had a very vivid dream which I shared with my wife, who stated that she confirmed in her spirit that it came from God. In this dream, the Lord told me that I would go to Eugene and that He would cause the branch office to prosper. God further told me that He wanted me to share His glory with the saints in a church in the north end of Eugene. He told me that the church building was new, that the exterior was faced with pink stone, that He would lead me to the church, and that He would use me among the people to help them learn to know the voice and ways of the Lord."

Already the people in the congregation were saying, "Amen, praise the Lord."

"At this point in my dream," he continued, "I was given an overall view of the city, as though flying over it in an airplane, and I saw that the main route to this church was lined with blossoming cherry trees. I saw the church building very distinctly. Then I awoke.

"In obedience to this dream and word from God, I came to Eugene on Friday," he said. "I've searched for two days for a branch location, and I think I have found one. This evening I was in the large downtown church when, in the midst of the song service, God spoke to me and said that I was not in the church He had showed to me in the dream and that I should get out of there immediately.

"Hesitantly, I obeyed," he said, "not knowing how to find my way across town, but the Lord directed every turn I made from that church to this one. I drove right up to the building, and I know I am in the center of God's will. I'm looking forward to becoming part of what God is doing here among you."

We were nearly hilarious with joy. We needed all the help we could get, but especially wanted someone who knew the voice and ways of God as confidently as he did; so we extended the right hand of fellowship to him and offered him every possible assistance in locating in Eugene.

The amazing part of this story is that, in the years that have passed since his visit, we never heard from him again. One wonders how, after God so supernaturally imposed His will upon that man's mind, he could ignore it so completely. Yet we dare not point fingers of scorn at him for we, too, have not always obeyed the known will of God. But this Psalm suggests that if we want to abide in God's presence, we must learn to do what He says, when we know He is speaking, even if the cost seems to be beyond what we had expected.

If God cannot trust what we say, He certainly is not going to allow us in on heaven's great secrets. He will just leave us in our religious isolation, contenting ourselves with the sayings of men. Jesus told His disciples, "If any man *will do* his will, he *shall know* of the doctrine . . ." (John 7:17, italics added). Obedience opens the flow of divine knowledge as surely as disobedience closes it. God does not speak in order to give us information upon which to base our choice of whether or not to obey; He demands obedience before He declares His will. When I am aware that God is no longer speaking to me, I check back to remember the last thing He told me to do and usually find that I have not fully obeyed. When I obey, He begins to speak again.

Yet, too frequently, when the emotions are stirred, we submit, but when the emotions are stilled, we vacillate. May God teach us to never doubt in the darkness what we trusted in the light.

The Jerusalem Bible translates this verse of Psalm 15: ". . . who stands by his pledge at any cost." It calls for consistency in the control of life. God made us to control ourselves through our will. Adam was created a free moral agent who was encouraged but not forced to obey God. God designed man to be governed from within, not from without. Unfortunately, Satan and much of religion seek to exert outer control over man, bringing him into slavery, but God works consistent to His original blueprints and places His Spirit within the spirit of man.

One of the first works of salvation is to restore man's free moral agency and to instruct man how to reign over every aspect of his life. Salvation releases a man's will to function as commandant over the soul and body. Throughout my years of pastoring I have repeatedly been called to hospitals by doctors who reported that a patient had lost the will to live. The doctors have explained that everything that could be done medically had been done and that there was good reason to believe that the patient would live if he really desired to live. If I could get that person to exert his will in authority over all the negatives in his life, he survived and mended quickly. This was not a situation of mind over matter but of will over emotion. The whole force of life requires direction, and God has determined that it should be in our will.

Genesis 1:26 tells us: "And God said, Let us make man in our image, after our likeness. . . ." This must refer, among other things, to the triune nature of God Himself. Paul says, "And the very God of peace sanctify you wholly; and I pray God your whole *spirit* and *soul* and *body* be preserved blameless unto the coming of our Lord Jesus Christ" (1 Thessalonians 5:23, italics added). Man is definitely a tripartite creation of spirit, soul, and body intricately interwoven until it is difficult to draw defined lines between them. But although there is complementary interaction among these components of man's nature, there is definite distinction as well.

The *spirit* motivates life. Man's will seems to be in the area of his spirit. It is in his spirit that man has a God consciousness or awareness. "The Spirit itself beareth witness with our spirit, that we are the children of God" (Romans 8:16). God's contact with man is not first intellectual but spiritual. Then man's spirit informs the intellect of the contact. It is from this will, located in man's spirit, that life's *motivation* flows.

The *soul* gives movement to life. Man's intellect and emotions are rooted in his soul from whence life gets its *movement.* A person can be an intellectual or highly emotional without being the least bit spiritual, for these are areas of the soul which are capable of operating quite independently from the spirit of man. It is in the soul that we have a self-awareness and a consciousness of others, but we never have a God consciousness in the soul level. God cannot be apprehended either by our mind or our emotions, but when our spirit contacts Him, both our mind and emotions become responsive.

The *body* gives manifestation to life. The actions of a man's life are manifested in his body. The spirit can direct the body to give *manifestations* of the will. The soul can also instruct the body to give expression of the intellect or the emotions. It is through the body that both spirit and soul can reveal themselves to others and give expression of worship to God. The body is more than the container; it is the revealer and the servant of the spirit and soul. God does not view the body as an unholy thing, but as the crowning glory of His creation.

The New Testament goes so far as to say that your body is the *temple* of the Holy Spirit (*see* 1 Corinthians 3:16, 17).

Perhaps three simple diagrams will help illustrate the interaction of our tripartite nature, depending upon what controls it. Since God made us to be controlled from the will, let's put it on the top of the pyramid as the capstone or the throne. That which is above all, controls all. This order fulfills God's original purpose for man. It allows the spirit to be in control, the soul to be available to both the spirit and body, and the body to be the slave of both. This is not only the way God created us, it is the order to which He

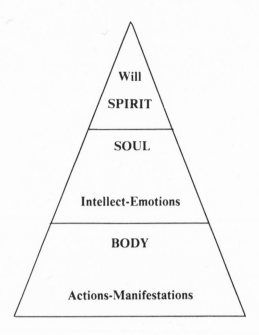

restores us when He recreates us. He has purposed that our area of God consciousness, the spirit, shall control the soul and body, for He commissions His Spirit to abide with us, in our spirit, to give us instructions for living.

However, the unregenerate man is basically unaware of his own spirit, much less God's spirit. He has abdicated the throne, and either his soul or his body reigns in his life. Those who have given themselves to the intellectual or the emotional control of their lives are ruled by their soul. A rather popular term is *soul power,* and it is accurate, for if the soul has control of the life, it has power indeed. We have all seen the tremendous power of the intellect which modern science displays, and most have also experienced the vast reservoir of strength locked in our emotional structure. God has given great energies to the soul, so much so that many confuse it with their spirit. Most religion is controlled from the soul level,

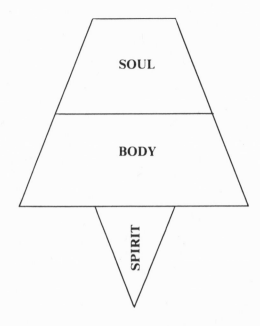

although many misinterpret it as spirit. It appeals either to the intellect with words and ritual, or to the emotions with music, art, and architecture. It has always interested me that whether the religious expression is emotional or intellectual, it is soulish, but the emotional disciples loudly condemn the intellectual approach to God, while the intellectuals, in their beautiful downtown church, despise the emotional worshipers in the suburbs. Each is misreading a different area of the soul and calling it spirit.

I have been in services where the worship has been beautifully soulish and have cringed as the leader referred to it as a "very spiritual worship." Conversely, I have been a guest speaker in services that were exquisitely intellectual and again have heard the leader refer to the service as "spiritual worship." It is not possible to have spiritual worship unless it comes through the spirit. The intellect and the emotions will function as part of the worship, but the direction must come from the spirit, not from the soul. But if the life is directed from the soul level, so will the worship. And no matter how polished and perfect the soul may become, it can never be spirit. This is why a study of the oriental religions is of no value to one who would really know God. Transcendental meditation, yoga, zen, and many other practices require concentrating great mental powers or exercising great control over the emotions, but none of these can contact God. The life that is lived under the control of the soul will never know the abiding presence of a living God.

There is still a third group of people in this world who are really upside down. They have allowed their body, with its appetites, passions, lusts, cravings, and pride, to dominate them. These include the athlete, the clotheshorse or fashion plate, the pleasure seeker, the drug user, the libertine, and all who are controlled by their body. I am, obviously, speaking in broad generalities and do

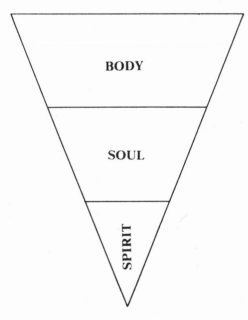

not intend this as a condemnation of athletics or the wearing of proper apparel. But when these things become the controlling force in our life, we are body directed instead of spirit directed. We are living according to the dictates of our animal nature instead of our eternal nature. These live by the philosophy that "if it feels good, do it." They find great fulfillment in displaying themselves either in prowess, possessions, or passions. They eventually discover that their body, which is a marvelous slave, is a terrible master.

This form of life control leads very easily to what the Scriptures call "ungodliness." Since this control of the life is totally physical, it tends to be a high form of animal life, totally locked into the dimension of time, and causes constant aging and decaying; so one must reach for whatever pleasure he can find at the moment. Lacking a concept of eternity, the ungodly also lack the deterrent to sinning that the spirit-controlled man has inherently.

The Gospels point out that this was the situation in the time of Noah and later in Lot's day. "They did eat, they drank, they married wives, they were given in marriage, until the day that Noah entered into the ark, and the flood came, and destroyed them all. Likewise also as it was in the days of Lot; they did eat, they drank, they bought, they sold, they planted, they builded" (Luke 17:27, 28). No amount of preaching or warning by men or angels could create a consciousness of righteousness, godliness, or impending judgment. They were so physically controlled that all they were concerned with was food, drink, sex, and commerce. It sounds quite modern, doesn't it? The person controlled by his soul at least has an awareness of eternity, but the body-controlled person rarely does.

So living concurrently in each of our communities are people controlled by separate levels of their life. Some are nearly animal-like; they are controlled by the dictates of their fleshly body. Others are controlled by their soul, whether the intellect or emotions, and the redeemed saints of God have been reinstated as spirit-controlled people. Little wonder, then, that society has such a difficult time legislating righteousness. Our laws treat men as though they were homogeneous while, in fact, we are multifarious not because of race but because of the area of control we have selected to rule our lives.

This helps explain why Jesus was so dogmatic when He said: "Except a man be born again, he cannot see the kingdom of God" (*see* John 3:3). The first prerequisite to entering into the limited area of God's Kingdom available to man while still here on earth is that he be changed to a creature that is controlled from the spirit level of his being. His will must control his life, and his spirit must be awakened before God will recognize him as a citizen of His Kingdom. God insists on connaturality in His Kingdom, and the first step in achieving it is to have all of its inhabitants controlled from their spirit level.

The second step in achieving this uniformity is for all who are controlled from their will to make a commitment of that will to God Himself. It has been so wisely said, "Our wills are ours to make them thine." God never purposes to violate or to remove our will. He merely wants us to submit that will to Him; to give Him the veto power over it.

In chapters four and five of his great book *Invisible War,* Dr. Donald Grey Barnhouse masterfully unfolds the truth that until the sin of Satan, there had been one will exercised in all of creation. Myriads of angels had so submitted their wills to God that there was only one effective will extant. God said: "Let there be . . ." and there was—without reservation, hesitation, explanation, or committee action. Then, according to Isaiah 14:12–15, Lucifer, the anointed cherub that covered the Ark, began to exert a second will into eternity saying five times, "I will." The exercise of his will was in direct competition and opposition to the will of God. He cried, "I will *ascend* into heaven, I will *exalt* my throne above the stars of God: I will *sit* also upon the mount of the congregation, in the sides of the north: I will *ascend above* the heights of the clouds; I will *be like* the most High" (italics added).

Barnhouse writes: "It is of extreme importance that we catch the transition which comes with the introduction of this second will. It is now manifest that eternity has taken on a new aspect or, to put it otherwise, that time is fully underway. The quality of eternity is the fact that there is but one will—the will of God. Then all was holy, all was righteous; there was no evil whatsoever. The quality of time is that there is more than one will. There came into the universe a second will, rising from the heart of Lucifer, the highest and most wonderful of all the created beings in the universe. In addition to the voice of God, there was now a second voice saying: 'I will . . .' There was rebellion; but, more important, back of the rebellion, there were two wills. That means conflict. It is possible to say that the shortest definition of sin is simply 'I will . . .' It makes no difference who speaks the words. The will of God is a line of truth and goodness that is unbending. It moves straight and with certainty across the universe of space, time, and thought. Any variation from that will of God, be it only in the slightest fraction of a degree, causes a tangent of separation and deviation—and that is sin. In the future the universe will get back to eternity; there shall be no more time, because there shall be no more deviation from the will of God. Christ shall put down all rule and all authority and power. For He must reign until He hath put all enemies under His feet (1 Corinthians 15:24, 25). Those of us in whom God plants eternal life are made partakers of the Divine nature, having escaped the corruption that is in the world through wanting one's own way (II Peter 1:4, Greek). We then are able to say from the heart that which no man who is not born again can say, namely, 'Thy will be done . . .' "

Although Satan was cast out of heaven, his plans never altered. He drew as many of heaven's angels with him as he could and set up headquarters in this earth region. When God placed man, with his powers of procreation, here on the earth, Satan schemed to gain control of God's heavens by causing man to surrender his will to him—to vote for his cause. He could see the billions of men, in ages to come, all under his control ultimately giving him sufficient power to override God's will. His first approach was to the woman, Eve, and by deception that caused her to think that she was doing something good for her husband and the children to come, he caused her to transgress. But Adam was neither seduced nor deceived. With eyes wide open, Adam followed Eve in her transgression in order to maintain the relationship they had enjoyed before Eve fell. Adam said, "I will eat of the tree" in deliberate rebellion against God; and his rebellion was as distinct and specific as was Satan's original rebellion.

Quoting again from *Invisible War,* Barnhouse continues, "Let us state it in a series of facts about the fall. Satan succeeded in detaching man from obedience to the Word of God. True. Satan also succeeded in detaching man from a belief in the goodness of God. True. Thereby, Satan won man away from confidence in God and dependence upon God. True. But though Satan won all of these victories, he lost the whole battle in the fact that he did not succeed in attaching man to himself.

"In the beginning there had been one will, the will of God, the Creator. After the rebellion of Lucifer, there had been two wills, that of God and the rebel. But *now there are billions of wills.* A significant verse in this connection is: 'All we like sheep have gone astray, we have turned every one to . . .' What? In the fact that we have gone astray, we read that we have all left the will of God. But in the turning away from God, did we all turn to Satan? Was it a mere change of allegiance? Was it like Italy, fighting with Germany in the Spring of 1943 and with the Allies in the autumn? Far from it. 'All we like sheep have gone astray, we have turned everyone *to his own way'* (Isaiah 53:6). This is the revealing statement. There are no longer two wills in the universe; there are more than two billion wills in this world alone.

"The sin of Adam was, in the final analysis, the echo of Satan's own declaration of independence. Satan had had a glimpse of the glory of God and wanted it for himself. 'I will be like the Most

High . . .' he cried. When Adam sinned, there was the same rebellion: 'I, too, will be like the Most High.' "

Satan now found himself in competition not only with the will of God but with the will of man. He does not automatically control a single person; each must be made to surrender his will to him. This has proved to be an awesome task. He has found man to be untrustworthy and fickle, and Satan must consistently entice or coerce that man to keep him surrendered.

This is why the spiritual battle the Christian finds himself engaged in is a conflict of wills. Satan attacks man's mind endeavoring to gain access to his will. The only power left him by Jesus for battling against the Christian is the power of persuasion, but it is formidable. He will entice, bribe, shame, project fear, and promise fame to get us to surrender our will to his desires. His approach will vary from that of the beautiful serpent to that of the roaring lion, but he is prevented from doing anything beyond persuading us until we bend our will to him.

When Satan was sorely tempting Jesus in the Garden of Gethsemane, Jesus prayed: "Father . . . not my will, but thine, be done" (*see* Luke 22:42). At that point, the temptation to bypass the cross ended. Temptation always ends when our will bends to God's will and Word. Satan continues to press only as long as he is aware that the saint has not yet surrendered the point to the will of God. As long as we are operating in our own will level, Satan feels he still has a chance to induce us to succumb to his will, but the moment we both realize that the cry of our spirit is that the will of God be paramount in our life in this issue, he will leave us alone, for he knows he has lost the battle.

It must greatly amaze Satan to see men and women turn from the exercise of their will to submission of their will to God for nothing more than love. It must astonish him to watch men walk away from their possessions and suffer privation and to leave their country to go to a foreign heritage to preach the Gospel for no other motivation than the love of God. No force, no threats, no overwhelming arguments—just divine love. He who seems to use fear and hate to control his legions finds it difficult to understand 2 Corinthians 5:14, "For the love of Christ constraineth us. . . ." The word *constraineth* is translated variously by other translators. Weymouth says *overmasters us.* Goodspeed writes *controls me.* The Twentieth Century New Testament puts it *compels us,* while the New English Bible says *For the love of Christ leaves us no choice.*

Then, the surrender of my will to the will of God is, not to be categorized with the surrender of my wallet to a gunman, but more like the surrender of two people to each other in the marriage ceremony. The force to which they surrender is love, and the motivation of the surrender is also love, but the act of surrender is *I will.*

I am grateful that in June of 1943 when Eleanor Louise Eaton stood by my side and heard my father ask her, "Eleanor, wilt thou have this man who stands by your side to be your lawful wedded husband, to have and to hold from this day forward?" she did not answer, "I think so," or "I feel like it." Her straightforward answer was, "I will." It was a lifetime commitment that had to come from something higher than the body or the soul; her very spirit opened its will to love and surrendered to be my wife for life.

So God moves upon us with His love to motivate us to make a lifetime surrender to Him, for He knows far better than we do how important it is for our will to be subservient to His will. He knows the will is the control force of the life. All guidance, all leadership, all decisions are in the will. It becomes the keel and the rudder of our life. And when that will is set inviolate to the will and Word of God, nothing can move us off course or deter us; the most Satan can do is slow us down with winds of adversity, but when the storm has subsided, we'll discover ourselves to still be in the center of the will of God.

Because redemption itself does not bring man's will into submission to the will of God but merely brings it into control of the man's life, God helps us submit our will to Him on a day-to-day basis.

The New Testament promises: "For it is God which worketh in you both to *will* and to *do* of his good pleasure" (Philippians 2:13, italics added). God commends His love *to* us and then by His Spirit works *in* us, making it desirable and pleasurable to surrender to Him. Inasmuch as the soul is the threshold of the will and, as such, often sets up a guardianship over it, God regularly informs the intellect and inspires the emotions in order to get to man's will. But the informing and the inspiring are not ends, only means to an end. All of the movings of the Spirit of God—His blessings, His instructions, His supernatural interventions into our affairs—are to enable Him to get to our will. God's church is neither an educational institution nor an entertainment center, but He does appeal both to our intellect through teaching of the Word and to our emotions through the ecstasy of the Spirit as part of the process to nudge our will into submission to His will. For God wants wills that are totally, unconditionally, unreservedly submitted to Him.

We know, for instance, that salvation is an act of the will. First, God willed to provide the salvation even before the foundation of the earth was laid (*see* 1 Peter 1:18–20). But receiving it is an act of man's will. Salvation is not an emotional experience, although many people get emotional while entering into this experience. Salvation is not merely a mental process, although the mind is gloriously renewed in Christ. It is an act of the will. If we will confess, He will convert.

Even a casual observance of the lives of most parishioners would suggest that far more people are convinced than converted. There has been more mental accommodation of the truth than there has been commitment of the will. There has been more forsaking of external sin than internal sin—the act of the self-will. More get emotionally involved with Jesus the Saviour than get identified with Jesus the Lord. More are sorry for sin than are submitted to Christ. If we are in control of our lives, it is obvious that Christ isn't and that we have still "turned every one to his own way" (*see* Isaiah 53:6). But true conversion does not come until there is an act of the will that changes the direction of the life.

It is equally true that continuing relationship with God is also an act of the will. As surely as the key to marriage is the pledging of "I do" one to the other, so the key to union with Christ is "I delight to do thy will, O my God" (*see* Psalms 40:8). This should not be subject to our changing emotions or enlarging intellect; it should be a settled act of the control center of our lives. "For better, for worse, for richer, for poorer, in sickness, or in health, and forsaking all others cleave I only unto thee" should be the pledge of our will to God if we would enter into a lifelong relationship of abiding with Him.

These commitments need not be constantly reaffirmed; they simply need to be honored. In my past experiences I have come forward in consecration services to reconsecrate what I had consecrated in a prior consecration service. What immaturity! Do I need to reaffirm my marriage vows to my wife monthly or even annually? Similarly, must I give my life to God over and over again? If it was genuinely given to God, there is no way I can get it back. How can I pry anything loose from God's hand? God wants us to come to the place where every willed submission is eternal. Psalm 15 puts it: "He that sweareth to his own hurt, and changeth not."

In Acts we see a fine example of this principle. Paul was headed towards Jerusalem because of a clear, confirmed word from the Lord telling him to do so. When his entourage arrived in Caesarea, they spent many days in the house of Philip, the evangelist, who had four daughters who were prophetesses. Toward the end of his stay, Agabus, a prophet, came from Judea and very dramatically took Paul's girdle from him and bound his own hands and feet with it prophesying, "Thus saith the Holy Ghost, So shall the Jews at Jerusalem bind the man that owneth this girdle, and shall deliver him into the hands of the Gentiles" (*see* Acts 21:11). This caused all present to plead with Paul not to go, just as the saints in other cities had done (*see* Acts 20:23). They interpreted God's prophetic utterance by their emotions rather than by God's Word and wanted Paul to escape the things God said would come to him. They misinterpreted forewarning of disaster as a call to flee from it. But Paul, far more mature in the ways of God than they were, simply pointed out that God had not said to avert the problem, only to be aware of it, and when they realized that they were tampering with the will of God that had just been expressed, they all said, "The will of the Lord be done" (*see* Acts 21:14).

How important it is that we stop saying what God's will is and start listening to what His will is. When God has expressed His will, we are to submit to it no matter what the cost may seem to entail. And cost us it will. No one has learned to walk intimately with God without paying a price. But the product is worth any price that can be asked of us.

"Abiding in the tabernacle" and "dwelling in the holy hill" are not to be equated with "getting high on Jesus." Abiding and dwelling are continuing experiences that are the result of a committed will. It will have its highs and its lows, its understandings and its misunderstandings, but the abiding relationship stands firm irrespective of the vacillations of the soulish nature or the health or sickness of the physical nature. "He that doeth the will of God abideth for ever" (*see* 1 John 2:17).

6

Adjusted Wealth
Aids Abiding

He that putteth not out his money to
usury, nor taketh reward against the innocent. . . .

A submitted will always pays the cost, even if it means a realignment of wealth. Remember that when the rich young ruler approached Jesus asking how to inherit eternal life, Jesus observed in quizzing him that he was a faithful keeper of the law but lacking in one thing—the proper handling of his riches. When Jesus touched his pocketbook, the man turned away and "was very sorrowful" (*see* Luke 18:23). He wanted entrance to God's Kingdom but was unwilling to share anything he possessed at the command of God. Isn't it amazing how often money is the separating wall between abiding and merely ascending?

It shouldn't be too surprising, then, that the fifth area of our lives that will need adjusting if we are going to be able to abide, not just ascend—to stay, not just stand in God's presence—is the way we handle our money. Psalms 15:5 says: "He that putteth not out his money to usury, nor taketh reward against the innocent. He that doeth these things shall never be moved."

God's Word says much about money and how it is handled. As a matter of fact, it is mentioned more frequently than many of the subjects that become the themes of books and sermons. His concern is rooted in the basic fact that money is you on deposit—you in a spendable form. When we exchange our brains and brawn for five dollars an hour, every five dollars in our possession represents an hour of our life. Harry Emerson Fosdick once wrote: "A dollar is a miraculous thing. It is a man's personal energy reduced to portable form and endowed with powers the man himself does not possess. It can go where he cannot go; speak languages he cannot speak; lift burdens he cannot touch with his fingers; save lives with which he cannot directly deal—so that a man busy all day downtown can at the same time be working in boys' clubs, hospitals, settlements, and children's centers all over the city."

Volumes have been written on the handling of money, but not too much has been said about God's expressed attitudes toward our finances. This fifth verse is consistent with the teaching of the whole Bible and seems to be concerned with acquisition of, attitude toward, and administration of money—or how we *get* it, how we *love* it, and how we *use* it.

Although it is written in the negative, its purpose is to teach a positive. It is concerned, first of all, with usury and, second, with bribery. Both concepts touch acquiring money in such a way as to hurt someone else. Fundamentally, all gains made by the wrongful loss of others is prohibited to the person who yearns to abide in the presence of God. To rob another for our own gain is always unscriptural, whether it is by taking a bribe to be a false witness, charging unfair interest rates to a distressed person, or any other method that defrauds another. There is a vast difference between making a profit and profiteering. It is the latter that is so condemned throughout the Scriptures.

There is a rarely used verse in the Bible that I have never heard quoted or preached. It says: "It is naught, it is naught, saith the buyer: but when he is gone his way, then he boasteth" (Proverbs 20:14). This is simply a matter of bartering the price down below the true value of the product by belittling it and pressing the seller with guilt. Having berated the seller to an abnormally low price, we brag to our friends about our cleverness. Although it gives the purchaser a great buy to boast about, the Word suggests that there was deceitfulness in the action. Whether we use a gun or guile, robbery is unscriptural. It may be legal, but in God's sight it is immoral. No matter how well one may stay within the letter of the law, taking what is rightfully another's will disqualify him from abiding in the presence of the Lord.

This does not apply exclusively to the clever lawyer who can switch the assets of an estate into his name without violating the letter of the law; it applies to the layman who cheats on his time card, defrauds on his income tax, or doesn't point it out when he has been given too much change. It is not the amount but the principle that counts. It is that inner desire to get what does not belong to us no matter who is hurt in the process. If we have to rob another to get it, we don't need it. The price of losing our standing in God's presence is too great to acquire wealth by cheating another.

But while this verse deals with acquiring money in the wrong way, elsewhere the Bible indicates the right way to earn money. Both the Old and the New Testaments declare: "There are six days in which men ought to work" (*see* Exodus 34:21; Luke 13:14). The principle of the Word of God is that man is to work to earn his living. When the curse was placed upon the earth because of man's sin, God told man that it would be by the sweat of his brow that he would wrest a living from the earth. Labor is God's provision for man's sustenance.

When Paul wrote his epistle to the church at Thessalonica, he found it necessary to say: "But we beseech you, brethren. . . . that ye *study* [Greek, 'be ambitious'] to be quiet, and to *do your own business,* and to *work with your own hands,* as we have commanded you; That ye may walk honestly toward them that are without, and *that ye have lack of nothing*" (*see* 1 Thessalonians 4:10–12, italics added). It would seem that even in his day there were some who had to be admonished to go to work. I guess that the concept that the world owes us a living isn't so new after all. Laziness is inherent in most of our natures, and unless we conquer it, it will control us. In a day when welfare, unemployment payments, disability insurance, and guaranteed income are so available, the lazy man can make a career of doing nothing and depending upon society to provide for him. We're all too aware of how great a rip-off this has become. But the Bible does not make society responsible for the lazy and indigent. It merely offers work for the able and aid for the poor.

Apparently, there were some Christians in Thessalonica who had a "welfare mind." In his second letter to the church, Brother Paul had to repeat the command to work for the third time. "For even when we were with you, this we commanded you, *that if any would not work, neither should he eat.* For we hear that there are some which walk among you disorderly, *working not at all,* but are busybodies. Now them that are such we command and exhort by our Lord Jesus Christ, that with quietness they work, and eat their own bread" (2 Thessalonians 3:10–12, italics added). The phrase "not working . . . busybodies" is a play on words in the original Greek language. Moffatt translates it: "Busybodies instead of busy," while William Neil translates it: "Stop fussing, stop idling, and stop sponging." How these words need to be heralded to some Christians of this generation who feel that their having accepted Jesus Christ as their Saviour automatically makes them the ward of the church. They claim to be "living by faith" when, in fact, they are merely sponging off working Christians.

The Bible teaches us to live by labor, not by faith, unless God clearly and confirmedly calls us into His special service. The God-appointed priests of the Old Testament were the only ones exempted from manual labor in the Old Testament; yet they were never idle. They worked long hours in the service of God and the tabernacle. God made no provision for idleness, for He who made us knows better than we that "an idle mind is the devil's workshop."

For years I taught the men of our congregation that unless they were turning out enough work for their boss to make a profit on their labors, they were stealing from their employer. They were not to merely put in their hours; they were to produce something in those hours. One man, who worked for the railroad and could get away with it, refused my teaching and told me, "I've informed my boss that I wasn't tired when I got on the job, and I don't intend to be tired when I leave it." I am afraid that his philosophy of work is far too widespread in today's labor market. One employer told me that he had to hire twelve men to find one who was willing to work. The others wanted a position, not a job.

Yet God's Word clearly says: "If any would not work, neither should he eat." This is not to condemn assistance for the needy, but to disapprove of laziness and the attitude that we have something coming to us without work on our part. Unearned reward is a silent mockery.

Consistently in counseling confrontations, I have been told, "I can't remain in God's presence and stay on the job." Yet the Bible seems to teach just the opposite—that you must stay on the job to remain in God's presence. Work—earning proper support for our families—is a divinely appointed task and is a prerequisite to abiding in God's presence. When we reject God's provision and seek the state's provision, we disqualify ourselves from God's presence and must substitute an association with society. When writing to Timothy, Paul spoke even more strongly than to the church at Thessalonica. He said: "But if any provide not for his own, and specially for those of his own house, he hath denied the faith, and is worse than an infidel" (1 Timothy 5:8).

"But," some may counter, "I am trusting God to supply my needs."

After more than thirty years in full-time Christian ministry, I can testify from my experience that God pays His laborers, but He only pays the ones He hires. Those who volunteer to do His work are not under His pay schedule. We shouldn't leave a job to do the work of the Lord unless He calls us off the job, as He did the twelve disciples. The seventy that He sent out two-by-two were not asked to quit their jobs but simply to go on a mission for Him between working schedules. Even Paul was self-supporting much of the time.

Does this invalidate the promise: "But my God shall supply all your needs according to his riches in glory by Christ Jesus" (Philippians 4:19)?

No! That verse follows an expression of thanks for a lavish gift they had sent for Paul's support while in prison. These were working people who were willing to share the fruits of their labors with God's servant. To them Paul offers the benediction of God's supply. When we've done all God commands us to do, we can expect Him to do the rest for us. But not until then!

Since Psalms 15:5 speaks first of the right and wrong ways to acquire money, it is to be expected that the second thing it would mention is our attitude toward the money we have acquired. The Psalm speaks of "his money." This sounds extremely possessive. It is not simply "money" or even "the money," but "*his* money." "It's mine!"

It's very easy to develop a possessive attitude towards money. I once had a church treasurer who felt that everything that came into the treasury was his and that he had to protect it from the preacher and other board members. He acted as though we were asking him to take money from his personal account for every needed appropriation in the church. He had become personally possessive of God's money.

Similarly, the controlling of the finances in the home is the number one cause for dissension and rates high as a reason for divorce. It is usually not the amount of money but the attitude toward the money that divides the home.

Therefore, the Scriptures teach us at least two controlling attitudes towards finance. First of all, don't love it; second, don't depend on it.

It is tragic to let money become the motivation of our life—the object of our love. This may be an American concept, but it certainly is not a divine principle. Since our new birth, we are Sons of God, we have the mind of Christ, and we have the Fatherhood of God; so we should embrace the divine concept, not the world's concept. Money is not to be our god or our motivation in life. It is better to have your bank in heaven than to have your heaven in a bank.

Perhaps few Scripture verses are more quoted than: "For the love of money is the root of all evil [literally 'a root of all kinds of evil']" but seldom do we hear the rest of the verse quoted: "which while some coveted after, they have *erred* from the faith, and *pierced themselves* through *with* many *sorrows*" (I Timothy 6:10, italics added). It is not possessing money but being possessed by money that becomes "a root of all kinds of evil." We're all too familiar with the multitude of stories of men who allowed themselves to become obsessed with a drive to make money. Morality and legality were set aside for expediency. Many times they succeeded in amassing fortunes but lost their families and often their freedom in the process. Many God-called men have forsaken the ministry in the pursuit of wealth, and countless thousands have refused to follow the Lord for the same reason.

This very attitude of covetousness will cause one to "err from the faith," and thereby disallow him from abiding in God's presence. "But without faith it is impossible to please him . . ." (Hebrews 11:6). The very first commandment given to Moses was: "Thou shalt have no other gods before me" (Exodus 20:3). When gold becomes our god and silver, our patron saint, we will abide in their presence having automatically banished ourselves from God's presence by our choice of other gods.

The man who serves the money god has dollar signs in the pupils of his eyes. Everything must turn a profit, or it is ignored. Of Jesus' day we read: "And the Pharisees also, *who were covetous,* heard all these things: and they derided him" (Luke 16:14, italics added). Did they deride Him because He preached a different doctrine? No! They derided Him because they were covetous. They couldn't see any monetary gain for themselves in being a disciple of Jesus; so they sneered at Him. The Revised Standard Version translates this verse: "The Pharisees, who were lovers of money, heard all this, and they scoffed at him." There are still many who say, "I-am-very-fair-I-see" (Pharisee) and scoff at the claims of Jesus Christ today, not because His claims are so unbelievable, but because they are so uncommercial!

This is also seen in the story of the rich young ruler. His love for possessions took precedence over his love for Christ. It is not that a vow of poverty is a prerequisite for a close relationship with the Lord, but all the possessives—my, mine, and our—must go. Dr. R.A. Torrey used to repeatedly remind his audiences: "Jesus Christ will be Lord *of* all or not Lord *at* all."

The man who allows his heart to develop a fixation for money will find himself in strange associations. The Bible says: "But fornication, and all uncleanness, or *covetousness,* let it not be once named among you, as becometh saints" (Ephesians 5:3, italics added). What miserable bedfellows! Fornication, uncleanness, and then covetousness. Does God see them as equals? Are they all unclean, destructive forces of equal potency? Apparently so, for they are put in juxtaposition by the Holy Spirit. All three are lustings of the flesh.

So we are clearly taught to earn money, but not to love it. "If riches increase, set not your heart upon them" (*see* Psalms 62:10). This is almost un-American. Our philosophy seems to be: "Love money, and use people to get it," while God's attitude is: "Love people, and use money to bless them." The Christian who will love what God loves (people) and use his temporal means to help, bless, and assist them will find a greater flow of material possessions than he had ever known before. When God sees that He can trust us with finances without their causing us to transfer our love from people to riches, He will abundantly bless us with prosperity so that we can channel it to the needy.

The second principle that will affect our attitude toward money is simply don't depend on it or trust it. It is possible to escape loving money and still fall into the trap of making it the source and center of our security. Psalm 52 speaks of an evil person full of treachery who God pledges to destroy, thereby causing the righteous to laugh mockingly. The righteous cry: "Lo, this is the man that made not God his strength; but trusted in the abundance of his riches, and strengthened himself in his wickedness" (v. 7). His wickedness was rooted in trusting in something short of God. His self-sufficiency made him a law unto himself; he neither needed nor feared God. Jesus knew well the deceitfulness of trusting in riches rather than God. He told His disciples: "Children, how hard is it for them that trust in riches to enter into the kingdom of God!" (*see* Mark 10:24). Note that He did not say, "them that *possess* riches" but *"trust* in riches." It is not rich men that are barred from entering into the Kingdom of God but men that trust in their riches. One need not be especially rich to trust in his finances. It is a matter of faith's object! The moment we begin to trust in riches, we no longer trust in God. To abide in God's tabernacle or dwell in His holy hill, our faith must be centered in Him continually, not merely during emergencies. We must see Him as the source of everything we need, even if we work with our hands in the process of getting it. In God's Kingdom He is the source of everything for all inhabitants. When we have another source, we have withdrawn from His Kingdom.

Furthermore, amidst the inflationary spiral the world is now experiencing, we have constant proof of the foolishness of trusting in riches. Yesterday's savings are nullified by tomorrow's increased prices. The ample retirement program carefully planned many years ago is but the barest subsistence in today's world. Obviously, our trust was not well founded.

How many families have been financially wiped out by one serious sickness! Hospitalization, doctor's fees, medicines, special nurses, therapeutic equipment, and sometimes legal fees (as in the case of an accident) can totally deplete a family's past savings and future earning power.

Some trust in their wealth, their bank accounts, and their gold, but we have been called to trust in our God. He gives, and He takes away, but He never leaves us or forsakes us.

But not only is Psalms 15:5 concerned with how we acquire money and our attitude toward that acquisition, it is primarily concerned with the way we administer that money. "He that putteth not out his money to usury. . . ."

Nearly all of the financial problems in American households are due to improper administration of the funds, not the insufficient amount of those funds. Most Americans have an income that would be considered lavish by the standards of the rest of the world. Yet a high percentage of these well-paid individuals are hopelessly in debt and barely make it from payday to payday. The high incidence of personal bankruptcies proves that many have little or no concept of a working budget.

Because an improper administration of our wealth so vitally affects our abiding in God's presence, we might do ourselves a favor to briefly consider four fundamental factors in the handling of our money.

First, we must learn to save it. An old Amish proverb says, "Spend less than you earn, and you'll never be in debt." That simple philosophy, if applied, would remove 90 percent of most Christians' worries. Indebtedness is a pledging of a life we have not lived in payment for things and services we've already used. It is what the government calls deficit spending, and it has become the American way of life. Credit cards, easy-payment plans, long-term credit for major purchases, and open accounts have encouraged us to mortgage our future to satisfy today's lusts. While it is argued that this is what has produced our present standard of living, it must also be accepted that it has produced ulcers, dependence upon sleeping pills, many broken marriages, and mental breakdowns. Credit is a wonderful thing and should be established by every responsible citizen, but improperly used, it can become a horrible taskmaster.

If Jesus were alive today seeking twelve disciples in America, He would undoubtedly experience greater difficulty in attracting them now than He did at Galilee. Although we might desire to respond to His bidding "Come, follow me," we would have to ask for ten years or so to get out of debt before we could go with Him. We have so mortgaged our future that we can hardly order our present.

Some years ago, the Lord began to deal with my wife and me to get on a cash basis. We doubled up on the few payments we had and finally liquidated all installments except the house payment. During this time our banker, who was an active member of our church, encouraged me to keep making car payments for the rest of my life, but to make them to a savings account. He referred to this as prepayment credit. We have done so for more than ten years and find that when a major purchase needs to be made, we have the cash with which to pay for it. Instead of credit costing us 12 to 18 percent, we have been paid a modest interest on our payments in the bank, and we are in a much better position to purchase at a discount by paying cash.

Shortly after we succeeded in getting on a cash basis, God began to send us to various countries around the world to minister. If we had been saddled with payments to make, we could not have gone. Now I do not have to look into my bank account to see if I can obey the Lord's directions in my life, for my future is not mortgaged. We maintain a modest savings account to make house payments, if necessary, and we are free to travel, preach, or do whatever He directs.

Both my wife and I can testify to the lessening of tension after we stepped to a cash operation. Although we have credit cards for convenience, we never charge anything unless we have cash in the bank to cover the charge.

This principle can apply no matter what the level of income. We must simply learn to live at a level a little lower than our income and save for the future instead of mortgaging that future. While we may have less possessions, we will have more peace. We may have to keep things longer and do some repairing instead of replacing, but it will release us from much worry and make us available to the service of the Lord. Someone put it quite simply: "When your outgo exceeds your income, your upkeep is your downfall." Reversed it could read: "When your income exceeds your outgo, the upkeep will have an overflow."

The second factor that should govern the handling of our money is that we must learn to tithe it. As distasteful as this subject is to the nontithing Christian, it is a principle written largely across the pages of God's Bible. It is not a provision of the law that was done away with in Christ, for tithing antedated the law by several hundred years. The principle and practice was merely codified in the law of Moses. The New Testament presupposes that a Christian gave the 10 percent that already belonged to God, and then taught about giving the tithe.

It is not my purpose to expound on the Scripturalness of tithing. There are many excellent books on this subject available in most Christian bookstores. I merely want to point out the Scriptural purpose of tithing and the place the tithe is designated to go. Violation of these provisions cuts short our time of abiding in the presence of the Lord.

One of the most explanatory passages in the Bible on this subject is Deuteronomy 14:22–27. I'll only give key excerpts from this passage, but I urge you to read it in its entirety in any translation you have handy.

It opens with a clear command to tithe. "Thou shalt truly tithe all the increase . . ." (v. 22). The next verse becomes very explicit in defining "all the increase." Everything that formed a profit or increase had an automatic "divine withholding tax" levied on it whether animal or vegetable, animate or inanimate. It was not considered a gift; it was God's "cut." It was viewed as tribute due the king or a licensing fee that permitted them to do business. Since all increase comes out of the life principle, and God is the source of all life, it is reasonable to return a small percentage of the increase to the One who made it possible.

But it may have been argued then, as it is often argued now, God really doesn't need the 10 percent, for the cattle on the thousand hills are His and all the gold and silver buried in the hills belongs to Him too. This is true. God doesn't need to receive our tithe; it is we who need to give it. The purpose of tithing has never been to keep God from bankruptcy; it is to enable us to discharge some of the tremendous sense of obligation and indebtedness we have toward God and to develop an honest sense of owing to Him.

The Living Bible translates verse 23 as: "The purpose of tithing is to teach you always to put God first in your lives." The more conventional translations simply say, "That you may learn to fear the Lord your God always." So the stated purpose of paying the tithe is to teach us, on a regular basis, that God is first and, therefore, gets the first portion of all of our increase: the paycheck, the garden, the interest on our savings accounts, our catch of fish, and so forth. Since money is me, the way I handle my money reveals much of my attitude toward myself. If I will not give God 10 percent of "me in a portable form" (money), it is very unlikely that I will give God a portion of me in any other form. No amount of singing "I surrender all" will convince God of our self-giving if we are repeatedly behind in our tithing. If we won't even give 10 percent, why should He expect us to give Him "all"?

How can we hope to stand in His presence on a continuing basis when we have refused to put God first in our lives? And if we cannot stand in His presence, there obviously can be no hope of our staying there in an abiding relationship.

Some years ago my father was conducting a water baptismal service in the church he was pastoring in Vallejo, California. He was a firm believer in baptism by immersion. As one man began to step into the baptismal tank, Dad noticed a huge bulge in his rear pocket and gently whispered: "Your wallet, Brother!" Ignoring the message, the man continued to descend the ladder into the water. Thinking that he had not heard him, Dad spoke loudly enough to be heard in the front row of the church, "Brother, you forgot to take your wallet out of your pocket."

"No I didn't," was his reply, "this is the part of me that needs to be baptized most."

It is not surprising that a few years later this man presented himself as a ministerial candidate and went out preaching the Gospel. He learned to put God first in his life by consecrating his filled wallet; it was easy, then, to give the rest of his life to the Lord in subsequent dealings of God.

While teaching us to put God first in our lives is the main purpose of tithing, it is not the only purpose. The second purpose is to make worship possible. No Hebrew ever came to God empty-handed. There was no way anyone could be a freeloader in Old Testament worship. If he didn't bring an animal, there could be no sacrifice. The people provided the meal offering, the wave offering, the peace offering, and so forth. Only the sin offering on the Day of Atonement was provided *for* them. All other presentations to God were provided *by* them. The priests offered the gifts in ritual; the people offered them in reality.

God was simply saying, "Let's be consistent about the method of worship. I'm offering you a sacrificial system so that there can be an involvement and an identification by you until the time that Christ comes and totally fulfills these types. But I am not going to provide the lamb, the ram, the turtledove, or any offering directly. I will give you an increase of the work of your hands; bring Me a tithe of that increase. If you are a shepherd, bring sheep. If you raise cattle, bring bullocks. If you're an orchardist, bring me the olives for oil; if you are a farmer, bring me the wheat. Bring me that which is an increase of you and offer it unto Me." No tithe —no worship.

Please remember that God required every Hebrew male to come to Jerusalem to appear before the Lord three times a year for the feasts of Passover, Pentecost, and Tabernacles (*see* Deuteronomy 16:16). In addition to these compulsory feasts, there were two additional optional feasts known as the Feast of Trumpets and the Day of Atonement.

For the great number of Jews who lived away from Jerusalem, this proved to be a formidable requirement. Who would feed them? Were they to become a burden on the brethren in Jerusalem? No! They were instructed to either bring their tithe or exchange it for money and bring the money to purchase whatever was needed for worship and for their sustenance while worshiping in Jerusalem (*see* Deuteronomy 14:25, 26).

So we can see that the third purpose of the tithe was to provide for their own needs while worshiping. Too often we think that everything brought before the Lord was destroyed by fire, but this was not so. The burnt offering was completely consumed by fire, but with the other offerings, the blood was merely sprinkled, the fat and entrails were burned, and the carcass was available to the priesthood and often to the sacrificer for food. The gifts they brought provided for the corporal needs of the worshipers—priests and people alike.

Similarly, we bring our "tithes into the storehouse, that there may be meat in mine house" (*see* Malachi 3:10) and from this we provide whatever we need for worship. We build buildings, buy pews, install organs, purchase hymnbooks, lay carpet, pay for utilities, hire janitors, provide for the pastor and staff members, and pay for a thousand other items that provide for comfort and convenience in our worship. This is the way we "eat" of the sacrifice that is brought in. It is paid for from the tithe that is first offered unto God, and then given by God to us to provide for us during our worship times together.

None of these items is necessary to God, and all of them could be dispensed with by man. We could worship without electric lights—thousands do every Sunday. We could dispense with pews, carpets, hymnbooks, air conditioners, and the like and still worship

God. But God graciously allows us to purchase anything we really desire to make worship more enjoyable, as long as we pay for it out of the tithe and offerings that are brought in. The total program of the church is to be supported by the total people in that church. And tithing is the most equitable way for all to share proportionally.

God has not only commanded us to tithe, He has also been very specific about where those tithes are to be paid. They are to go to "the place which the LORD thy God shall choose to place his name" (*see* Deuteronomy 16:6; also 14:23, 24, 25). In the Old Testament, no sacrifice could be offered unto God away from the tabernacle or temple. Tithing was not simply the setting aside of a tenth but bringing it to the God-appointed priesthood to be offered before the presence of the Lord.

A notable departure from this commandment was in the making of the golden calf. Gold, which should have been used in the construction of God's tabernacle, was brought to Aaron to be cast into an idol as a symbol of worship. God's judgment, realized through Moses, was the total destruction of the idol by grinding it to powder, burning it, strewing it on the water, and forcing the people to drink the water. All their sacrificial giving was lost.

Unless our gifts are given to a place where God has placed His name, they may very well go to construct another golden calf. So much money that is raised for religious purposes goes to people and projects that have never had the name and nature of God conferred on them by God. Using the name of God is not synonymous with having God place that name upon us. His name is given to His son and His bride, but not to His workmen. Christians would do well to check to see if it is really His house or merely an organization before presenting their tithes, for the command is to "Bring ye all the tithes into the storehouse, that there may be meat in mine house . . ." (Malachi 3:10). If it isn't His house, He won't be there to receive it; so although it was lovingly given, it was not received. It was missent and never forwarded.

For one whose goal is to abide in God's tabernacle, the tithe will always be given where God and His people assemble, for they will not want consistent fellowship in any other religious circumstance. To them worship requires the divine presence, and they will search the community to find the place where God has placed His name in this generation. That is where they will worship, eat spiritual food, drink spiritual drink, and find fellowship and spiritual direction; so that is where they will place their tithe. They long ago learned the impropriety and illegality of eating at McDonald's and then driving to Hardees to pay the bill. We pay where we eat. So having carefully searched for a church where God has chosen to place His name, they bring their tithes to that storehouse to provide whatever is necessary for the continuance of the ministry in that place.

Still a third fundamental factor in the handling of our money is that we should learn to give it. Israel had a second tithe which supported the priesthood and every third year, a third tithe was distributed among the poor (*see* Deuteronomy 26:12). Giving is the very heart of Christianity. "For God so loved . . . he gave . . ." (John 3:16). Liberality is a required characteristic of saints. It is inconsistent to speak of stingy saints. We may have stingy church members, but not stingy maturing saints. The more we imbibe the nature of God, by being in His presence, the more self-giving we become.

Paul urged the saints in Rome: ". . . that ye present your bodies a living sacrifice, holy, acceptable unto God, which is your reasonable service" (Romans 12:1). Is this a call for everyone to enter into full-time ministry? Of course not! The context would prohibit that interpretation. He is merely saying that while some present their bodies to the full-time ministry of God's Word, others present their bodies to an employer for money. That money, then, represents them. When they give a portion of that money, it is equal to their giving that much of their bodies to the service of God. They are actually giving themselves to God. That is what an offering really is—an opportunity for the worshiper to give of himself to the work of the Lord.

Obviously, the giving must be beyond the tithe for that belonged to the Lord in the first place. All offerings unto the Lord must come out of the remaining 90 percent.

In the New Testament, the true principle of giving is not tithing, but totality—everything we have belongs to the Lord. We are urged to be faithful stewards of all that we possess, recognizing that we belong to the Lord. Paul put it: "Ye are not your own" (*see* 1 Corinthians 6:19). "Ye are Christ's" (*see* 1 Corinthians 3:23). "The body is . . . for the Lord; and the Lord for the body" (*see* 1 Corinthians 6:13). Happy is the man who has learned that he belongs to the Lord—spirit, soul, and body—and, therefore, everything he possesses is subject to the call of the Lord. If he has $1,000 in the bank, and the Lord requests $100, he automatically has only $900 in the bank. There is no argument, no fanfare—just an automatic transfer from his account to the Lord's account. This man has learned "to present his body a living sacrifice" and will have little problem presenting himself before the Lord in an abiding, worshipful relationship.

There is still a fourth factor in the handling of our funds that affects our abiding relationship with God, and that is to learn to prepare for the future use of our money. Money on deposit is us. Someday our bodies will die, and our spirit and soul will go to heaven. What use will be made of that part of us still on deposit in our estate? Will we be dragged into the courts as heirs fight over the estate, or will we have already made a deposition of the funds through a will? Does that will provide for continued giving to the work of the Lord or is it merely given to loved ones?

Joseph made commandment concerning his bones before he died (*see* Genesis 47:30). He reminded the children of Israel of God's promise to return them to the land of promise, and he wanted his bones to go with them in that glorious Exodus. He wanted to be part of the future move of God and made preparations for it. So can we. Whatever part of us is left over after our life has been lived can be invested in God's work through wills, bequests, and gifts. But if we don't deliberately make such provisions, it is possible that the deposit of our life left here on earth will be wasted, as far as the work of the Lord is concerned.

It has been a source of sorrow to my heart to see how often the assets of a godly man fall into the hands of the ungodly to be prostituted. One outstanding radio minister died, leaving a Christian radio station to his heirs. They sold it to a firm that made it into a rock-'n'-roll station. If this man of God was allowed to know this in heaven, it must have broken his heart. He had not made provision for the work to continue after his death.

The one who yearns to abide in the presence of God will not live his whole life thinking about the now. He will involve himself in the future as well, confident that since he came into an abiding relationship, he became a creature of eternity filled with eternal life. In eternity, tomorrow is part of today, and today is part of tomorrow; so he will plan all of his financial investments with eternity's values in view.

Must money separate us from God? No! Quite the opposite. Properly earned, faithfully tithed, judiciously spent, and freely given, money, which is nothing more than another form of ourselves, can bless our union with God and undergird our standing in His presence. To the faithful steward was given the commendation: "Well done, thou good and faithful servant: thou hast been faithful over a few things . . . enter thou into the joy of thy lord" (*see* Matthew 25:21). Faithfulness in the things committed to him opened the door to the joys of the divine presence. So it shall ever be.

7
Abiding Assured

He that doeth these things shall never be moved.

What awesome assurance is afforded us in the final words of this Psalm: "He that doeth these things shall never be moved." Never forced to step out of the tabernacle; never asked to move out of God's holy hill. Hallelujah! This is precisely the promise given to the overcomers in the church at Philadelphia: "Him that overcometh will I make a pillar in the temple of my God, and he shall go no more out . . ." (Revelation 3:12). It is the ultimate in security. This is absolute assurance of abiding in God's presence. It is the everlasting access that the angels have enjoyed from the beginning but man has lost through sin. Now through a Saviour and adjusted behavior, man is welcomed back into the presence of God to stand before Him continually.

David the king realized the availability of this access when he wrote: "I will abide in thy tabernacle for ever: I will trust in the covert of thy wings. . . .[The king] shall abide before God for ever. . . . So will I sing praise unto thy name for ever . . ." (Psalms 61:4–8). Countless saints have found the reality of this abiding. They have learned to adjust their lives so as to be acceptable in heaven's courts. They accustomed themselves to God's authority over their lives and soon found themselves enjoying the realities of God's Kingdom while still living here on earth.

God's presence is not merely available in the hereafter. It is a reality in the here and now. Access to the presence of the Father has been made available to us while we are still locked into our time and space dimension. For some, the access will merely be momentary and of a crisis nature. For others, the foretaste creates a taste for and they begin a change in living patterns that enables them to abide continuously in God's presence.

"He that walketh uprightly, and worketh righteousness, and speaketh the truth in his heart. . . .sweareth to his own hurt, and changeth not. . . .putteth not out his money to usury . . . He that doeth these things shall never be moved."

Never be moved—from what?

First of all, that man will never be moved from the protection of Almighty God. The beautiful Psalm 91, which depicts the safety of the believer, begins by saying: "He that dwelleth in the secret place of the most High shall abide under the shadow of the Almighty" (v. 1). The allusion is to the holy of holies in the tabernacle, which was God's dwelling place. The inner hanging, which formed the ceiling, was pure white linen on which were embroidered cherubim angels with their wings outstretched; it was identical to the veil which separated the holy place from the holy of holies. These mighty angels are guardians of God's holiness in heaven. When the High Priest came into God's compartment on the Day of Atonement, trembling in fear lest God's wrath consume him, he was surrounded and encouraged by this great typical display of cherubim guardians. He had moved from the insecurity of the outer court to the invincibility of God's inner court. The wall between him and the outside and the ceiling between him and heaven were filled with God's protecting ones. What need did he have of fear while dwelling in such a secret place of security?

There is no greater protection than is afforded in the presence of God. All of heaven's resources and personnel are available for the defense of the abiding one. The closer we get to God, the less concern we need have for enemies. When Jesus grieved over the city of Jerusalem, he said: "O Jerusalem . . . how often would I have gathered thy children together, even as a hen gathereth her chickens under her wings, and ye would not!" (Matthew 23:37). God's ultimate protection is not in massed armies but in outstretched wings. He defends us by hiding us close to Himself in the hour of danger. When we are safely tucked under His wings, nothing can touch us until it has destroyed Him, and try as he will, even Satan has been unable to destroy Christ.

The second beautiful benefit that the abiding man will never. be moved away from is the personal communication of the voice of God.

God told Moses that He would commune with him from between the faces of the two golden cherubim upon the mercy seat that formed the lid of the ark of the testimony (*see* Exodus 25:22). Moses had to go into the presence of the Lord to communicate with God, for divine communication takes place in the midst of the divine presence. Those who try to hear the voice of God from the brazen altar are always disappointed, for He does not speak from the outer court but from the holy of holies.

Jesus assured us:: "If ye abide in me, and my words abide in you, ye shall ask what ye will, and it shall be done unto you" (John 15:7). The key to answered prayer, then, is to be in such an abiding place that communication is really taking place. The man who has made sufficient adjustment as to find an abiding place in God lives in constant communication with his God. The spirit within him maintains an open line to the Spirit within God for two-way conversations. He hears heavenly things and is allowed to speak of earthly matters. No one can ever move him from this privilege.

Still a third bonus of abiding is fruitbearing. Jesus taught us: "Abide in me, and I in you. As the branch cannot bear fruit of itself, except it abide in the vine; no more can ye, except ye abide in me. . . .He that abideth in me, and I in him, the same bringeth forth much fruit: for without me ye can do nothing" (John 15:4, 5). So much of our life has been unfruitful no matter how hard we struggled to bring forth an abundant harvest. But here Jesus tells us that the secret of productivity is not attempting but abiding. Dwelling in intimate relationship with Him will bring forth spiritual fruit as surely as the branch bears the fruit of a healthy vine. There can be no true fruit until we learn to abide in Him, and then there can be no stopping of the fruitbearing. The abiding man shall never be moved from productivity.

An exciting fourth benefit of abiding in Him is participation in the joy of His presence. In one of his moments of ecstasy, David wrote: "In thy presence is fulness of joy; at thy right hand there are pleasures for evermore" (*see* Psalms 16:11). Heaven is a joyous place. Jesus spoke much of joy and promised it to His disciples on several occasions. Paul spoke often of rejoicing,, and John reveals in the Book of Revelation that all the saints in heaven are filled with rapturous joy. How could we conceive of God's holy habitation as being anything less than a place of complete, perfect, and abounding joy? So great is this joy that it could be written of Christ: "Who for the joy that was set before him endured the cross, despising the shame, and is set down at the right hand of the throne of God" (*see* Hebrews 12:2). Knowing the nature of the joy of heaven, Jesus endured anything and everything to hasten His return into God's presence. But we need not wait until we get to heaven; the joy is a by-product of being in the presence of God. That joy, at least as much as our earthly bodies can stand, is available to the one who has learned to abide in God's holy hill. Such a person shall never be moved from the divine joy.

Perhaps the list of the things from which the abiding man can never be moved would outline another book, but certainly we must consider that one who has attained an abiding relationship with God can never be moved from participating in worship. That is the stuff of which heaven is made. All who get close enough to God engage in worship regularly. It is the answer of man's spirit to the divine Spirit of God. It is an outpouring of our love for Him in nearly inexpressible ways. It is the reason man was made in the first place; yet sin so locked him up that he could not release that worship. Coming into the divine presence on a regular basis unlocks the fountains of the deep until, "Deep calleth unto deep at the noise of thy waterspouts: all thy waves and thy billows are gone over me" (Psalms 42:7).

Until I came into an abiding relationship with God, I had been a frustrated worshiper. I could sing and praise, but I could not really worship. But as I learned to dwell in God, I found worship becoming a second nature to me. It was as natural as responding to the tenderness of my wife. It was fulfilling and gloriously satisfying. While praise so often was an effort controlled by my will, I found worship to be a nearly spontaneous response of my spirit to God when in His presence. Nothing can ever move the abiding one from participating in the exhilarating worship of God the Father, God the Son, and God the Holy Spirit; so let us abide!